PIANO · VOCAL · GUITAR

THE WEEKND
STARBOY

T0088809

ISBN 978-1-4950-8941-1

7777 W. BLUEMOUND RD. P.O. BOX 13819 MILWAUKEE, WI 53213

In Australia Contact:
Hal Leonard Australia Pty. Ltd.
4 Lentara Court
Cheltenham, Victoria, 3192 Australia
Email: ausadmin@halleonard.com.au

Visit Hal Leonard Online at
www.halleonard.com

STARBOY

Words and Music by ABEL TESFAYE,
GUY-MANUEL DE HOMEM-CHRISTO,
THOMAS BANGALTER, HENRY WALTER,
MARTIN McKINNEY and JASON QUENNEVILLE

PARTY MONSTER

Words and Music by ABEL TESFAYE,
MARTIN McKINNEY, ELIZABETH GRANT,
AHMAD BALSHE and BENJAMIN DIEHL

I'm good, I'm good, I'm ___ great. Know it's been a while, now I'm mix-ing up the drink.

I just need a girl who gon' real-ly un-der-stand. I just need a girl who gon' real-ly un-der-stand. ___

I'm good, I'm good, I'm great. Know it's been a while, now I'm mix-ing up the drink.

Recorded a half step higher.

I just need a girl who gon' real-ly un-der-stand. I just need a girl who gon' real-ly un-der-stand. {And I / I've been

seen her get rich- er on the pole. I _____ seen her, __ I knew __ she had to know. __ I've __
pop-pin'. Just took __ three in a row. I'm __ down to do it a - gain, I'm on a roll. ___ I've __

_____ seen her __ take down __ that te - qui - la, down by the li - ter. I knew __ I had to meet her. Ooh,
_____ seen him __ out - side, __ try'n' to reach her. You try'n' to leave him. You said __ I am the rea - son. Tell __

_____ she mine, ooh, girl, __ bump and grind. Ooh, __ she mine, ooh, girl, __ bump a line. ___ An -
_____ me lies, ooh, girl, __ tell me lies. Say __ you're mine. I'm yours for the night. __ I'm

Woke up by a girl. Don't e-ven know her name. Woke up by a girl. I don't e-ven know her name.

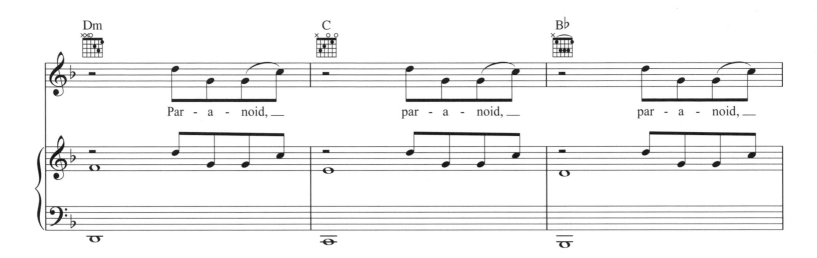

Par - a - noid, — par - a - noid, — par - a - noid, —

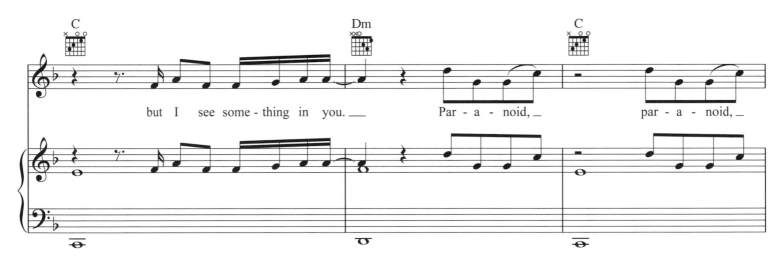

but I see some-thing in you. — Par - a - noid, — par - a - noid, —

par - a - noid, but I see some-thing in you. —

FALSE ALARM

Words and Music by ABEL TESFAYE,
HENRY WALTER, MARTIN McKINNEY,
AHMAD BALSHE, EMMANUEL NICKERSON
and BENJAMIN DIEHL

Recorded a half step higher.

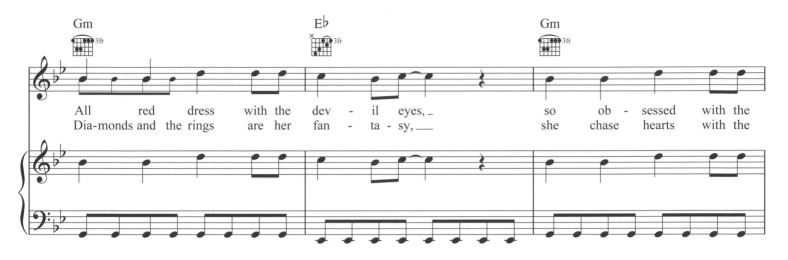

All red dress with the dev - il eyes, _ so ob - sessed with the
Dia-monds and the rings are her fan - ta - sy, _ she chase hearts with the

cam - 'ra lights. _ You love her, but you can't de - ny _ the truth, _
Hen - nes - sy. _ You love her, but you'll nev - er be _ e - nough, _

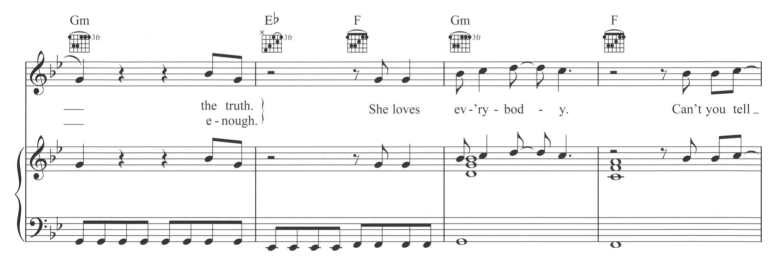

_ the truth. } She loves ev - 'ry - bod - y. Can't you tell _
_ e - nough. }

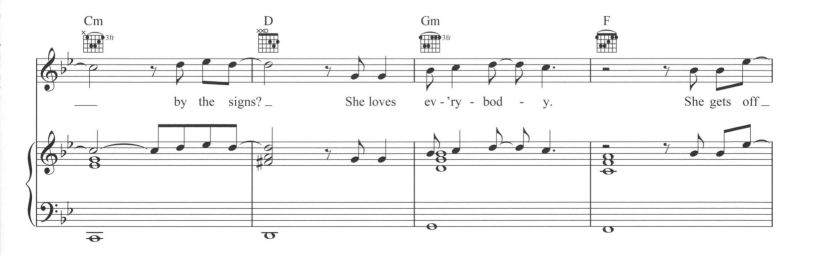

_ by the signs? _ She loves ev - 'ry - bod - y. She gets off _

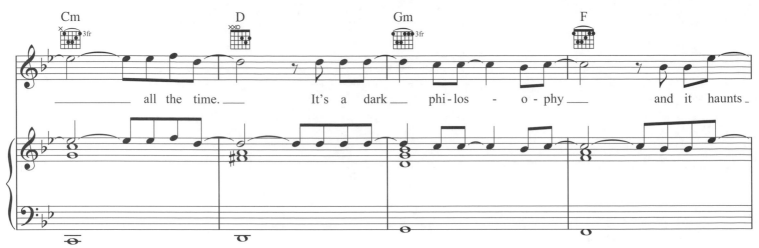

all the time. It's a dark phi-los - o-phy and it haunts

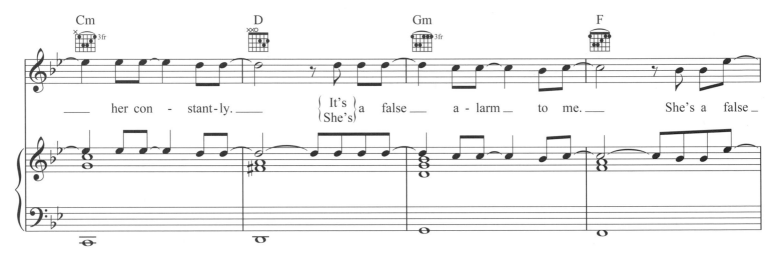

her con - stant-ly. {It's / She's} a false a - larm to me. She's a false

a - larm. False a - larm, hey, hey, hey, hey, false a - larm,

hey hey hey hey, false a - larm, hey, hey, hey, hey, hey.

False a - larm, hey, hey, hey, hey, false a - larm,

hey, hey, hey, hey, false a - larm, hey, hey, hey, hey, hey.

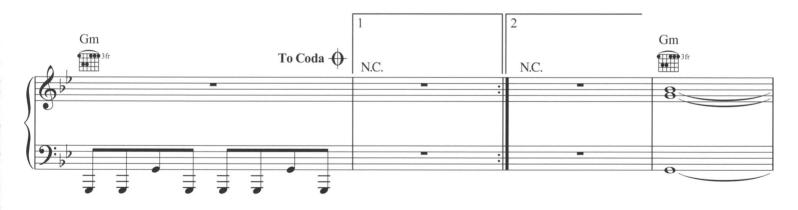

To Coda

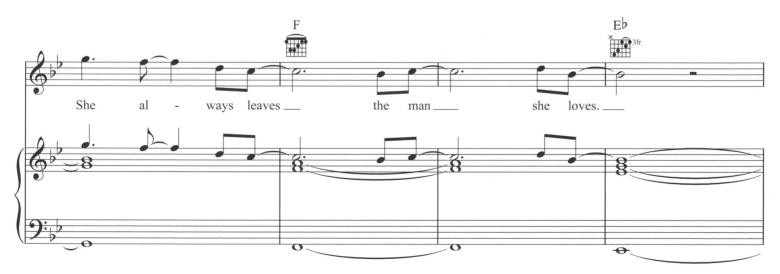

She al - ways leaves the man she loves.

REMINDER

Words and Music by ABEL TESFAYE,
HENRY WALTER, MARTIN McKINNEY,
EMMANUEL NICKERSON, DYLAN WIGGINS
and JASON QUENNEVILLE

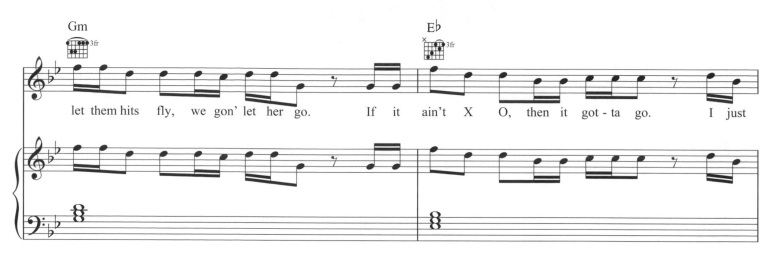

let them hits fly, we gon' let her go. If it ain't X O, then it got-ta go. I just

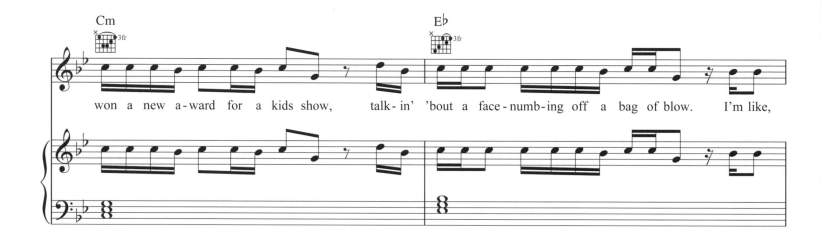

won a new a-ward for a kids show, talk-in' 'bout a face-numb-ing off a bag of blow. I'm like,

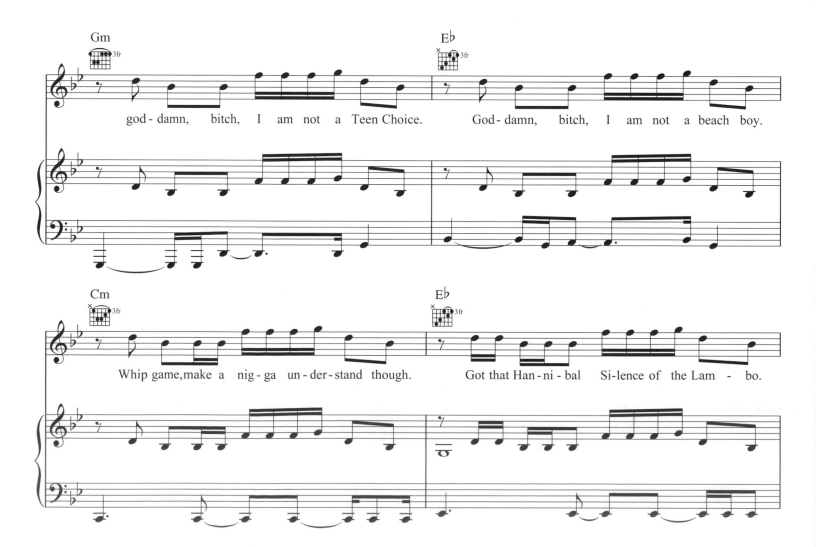

god-damn, bitch, I am not a Teen Choice. God-damn, bitch, I am not a beach boy.

Whip game, make a nig-ga un-der-stand though. Got that Han-ni-bal Si-lence of the Lam - bo.

try to for-get who I am, I'll be right there to re-mind you a-gain you know me, ___

you know me. ___ Said

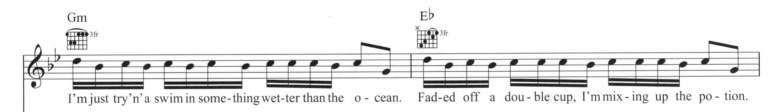

I'm just try'n'a swim in some-thing wet-ter than the o-cean. Fad-ed off a dou-ble cup, I'm mix-ing up the po-tion.

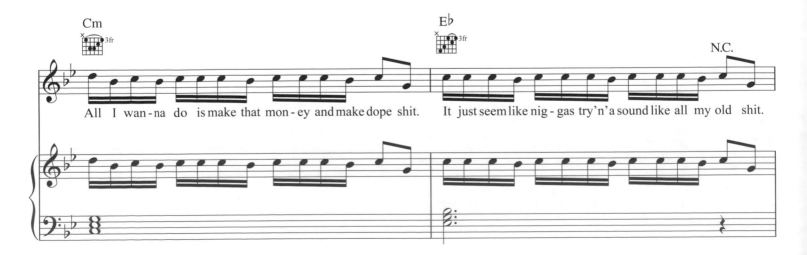

All I wan-na do is make that mon-ey and make dope shit. It just seem like nig-gas try'n'a sound like all my old shit.

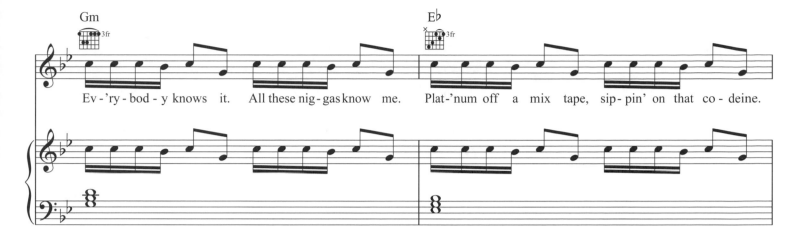

Ev-'ry-bod-y knows it. All these nig-gas know me. Plat-'num off a mix tape, sip-pin' on that co-deine.

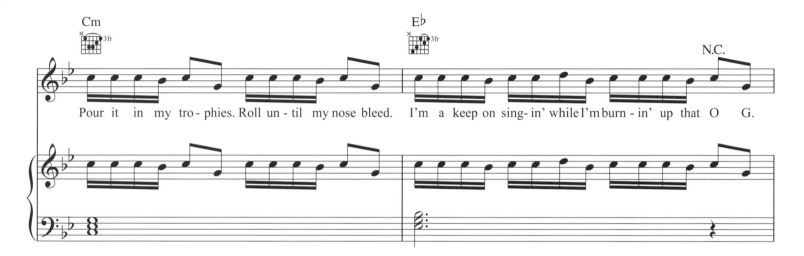

Pour it in my tro-phies. Roll un-til my nose bleed. I'm a keep on sing-in' while I'm burn-in' up that O G.

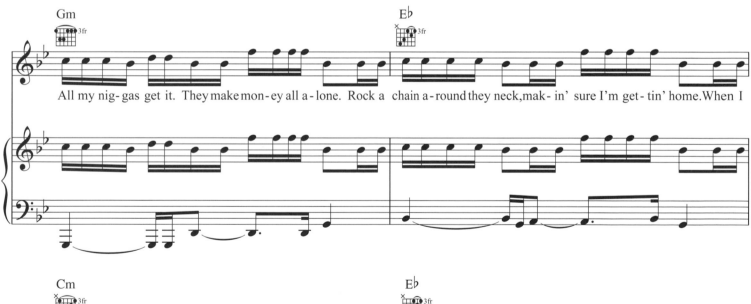

All my nig-gas get it. They make mon-ey all a-lone. Rock a chain a-round they neck, mak-in' sure I'm get-tin' home. When I

trav-el 'round the globe, make a cou-ple mil a show and I come back to my cit-y, I fuck ev-'ry girl I know. Used to

try to for-get who I am, I'll be right there to re-mind you a-gain. You know me, __

you know me, __ Why don't you

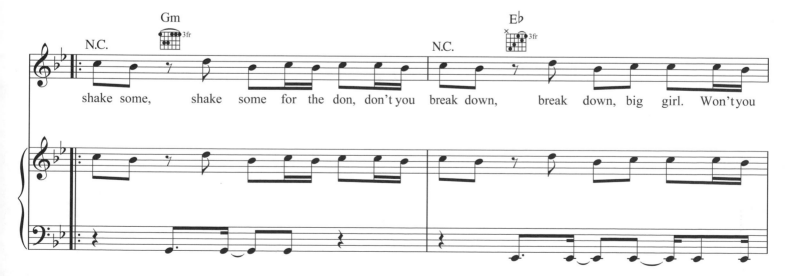

shake some, shake some for the don, don't you break down, break down, big girl. Won't you

work some,   work some for the don. Don't you hurt none,   hurt none. Big girl, won't you

hurt none,   hurt none.   'Cause you know me. _____   Do you

know me?   You know me. _____   Yeah, you

know me.

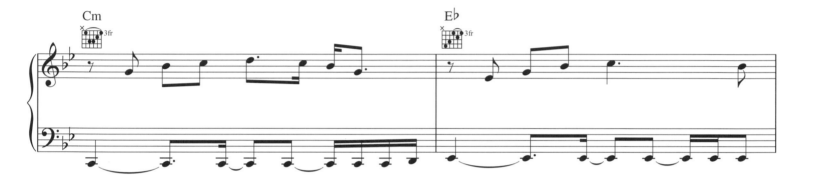

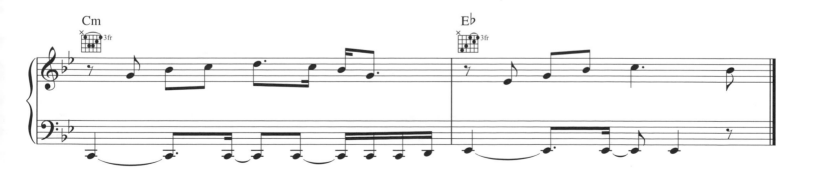

ROCKIN'

Words and Music by ABEL TESFAYE,
MAX MARTIN, ANDERS SVENSSON,
SAVAN KOTECHA, ALI PAYAMI
and AHMAD BALSHE

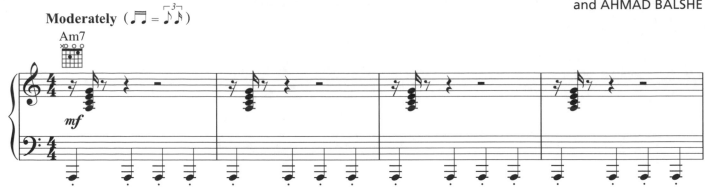

People al-ways talk a-bout the ones that got a-way.

I just seem to get the ones that al-ways want to stay.

Noth-in's gon - na stop me, I'm a get it eith - er way. Yeah,

oh, yeah.

Why would you wan - na take a - way from this mo -

- ment? We can own it.

Why would you want to take a - way from this mo -

- ment? You don't have to spend your life with me.

You don't have to waste your en - er - gy. We can just be

Dm7

rock - in', yeah, we can just be

rock - in', _____ yeah. _ I just want your

Am7

bod - y next to me. 'Cause it brings me so ___ much ec - sta - sy.

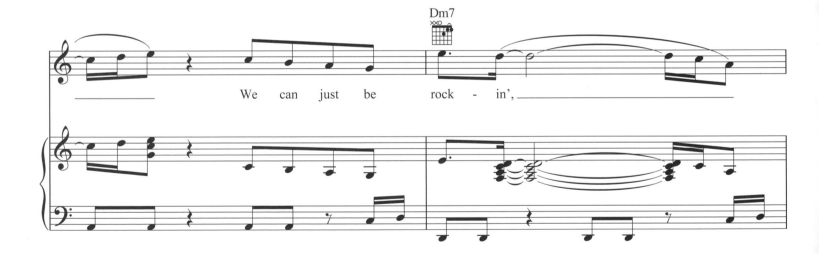

Dm7

_____ We can just be rock - in', _____

To Coda ⊕

yeah, _ we can just be rock - in', _____

yeah, _ yeah, _ yeah. _ You see me text - in', ba - by.

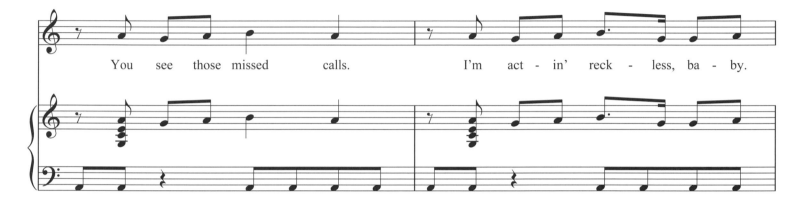

You see those missed calls. I'm act - in' reck - less, ba - by.

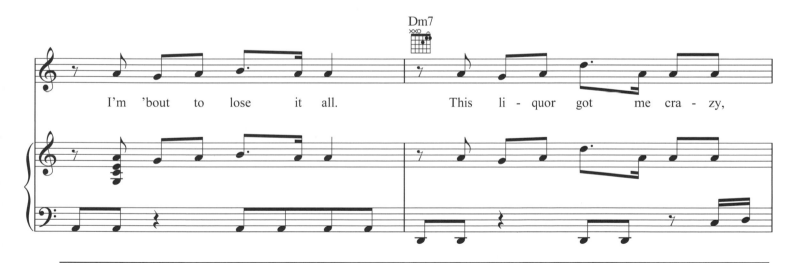

I'm 'bout to lose it all. This li - quor got me cra - zy,

mixed with that ad - der - all. ___ I'm fo - cused on ___ the ___ beat. ___

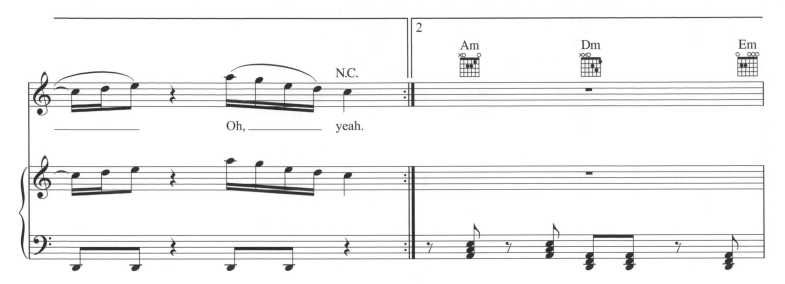

Oh, _____ yeah.

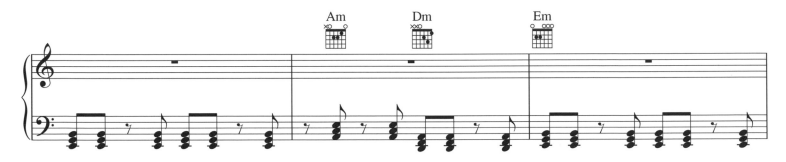

Oh, _____ tell you 'bout _ a Chi - na girl, _ 'bout a Chi -

- na girl, _ 'bout a Chi - na girl. _____

Oh, tell you 'bout a Chi - na girl, 'bout a Chi -

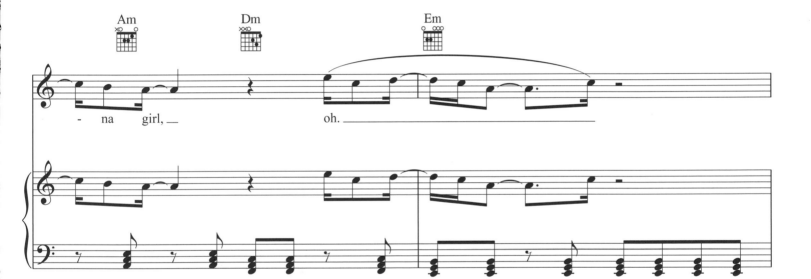

- na girl, oh.

N.C. **D.S. al Coda**

You don't have to

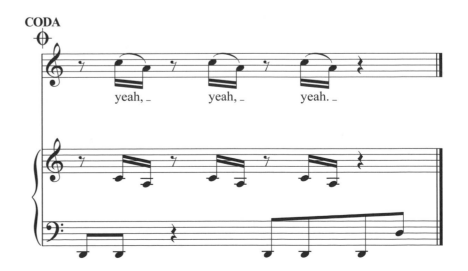

CODA

yeah, yeah, yeah.

SECRETS

Words and Music by ABEL TESFAYE, HENRY WALTER,
MARTIN McKINNEY, DYLAN WIGGINS, GEORGE CANLER,
JIMMY MARINOS, MIKE SKILL, PETER SOLLEY,
WALTER PALAMARCHUK and ROLAND ORZABAL

Moderately fast

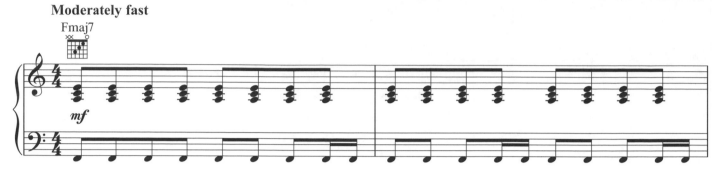

Ev - 'ry - bod - y here wants you, my

love, my love. _____

And I know that you want them, too, my

love, my love. _____

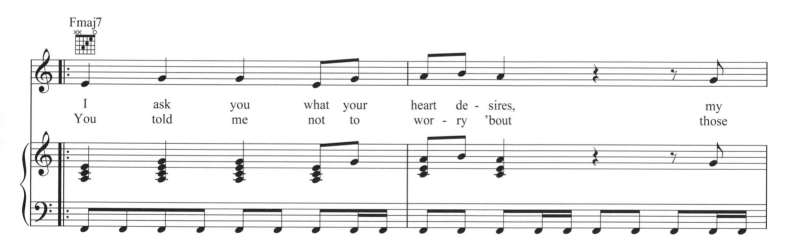

I ask you what your heart de - sires, my
You told me not to wor - ry 'bout those

love, my love. _____
guys, those guys. _____

You tell me I'm the on - ly one, my
You told me that you left it all be -

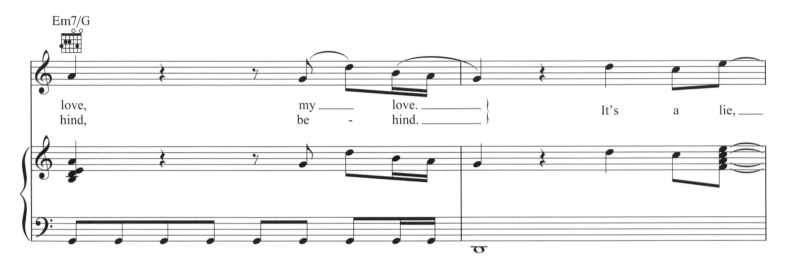

love, my love. It's a lie,
hind, be - hind.

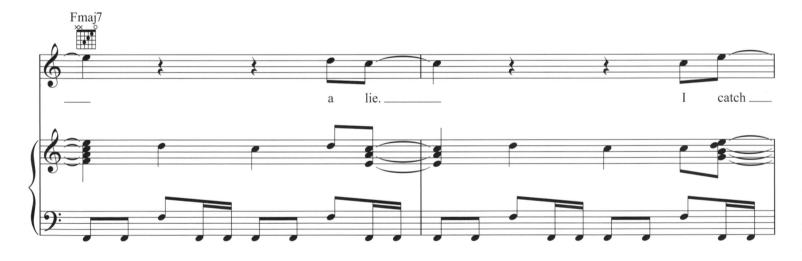

a lie. I catch

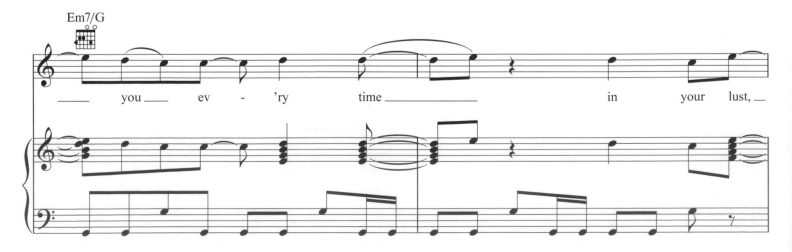

you ev - 'ry time in your lust,

your lust,_____ ev - 'ry time_____

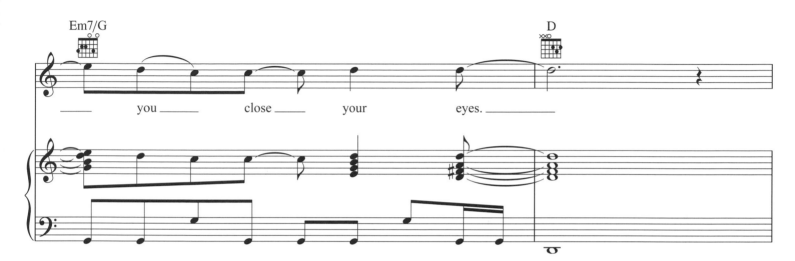

____ you _____ close _____ your _____ eyes. _____

I hear the se - crets that you keep _____

when you're talk - in' in your sleep.

I hear the se-crets that you keep,_____

keep,_____ keep when you're talk, talk-in',_____ talk-in'.

I hear the se-crets that you keep_____

when you're talk-in' in your sleep.

I hear the se-crets that you keep, _____

keep _____ when you're talk, talk - in', talk - in'.

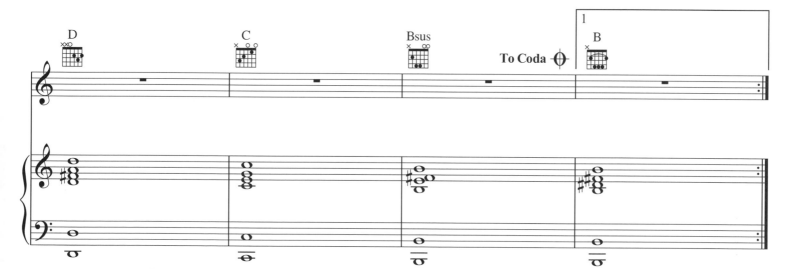

To Coda

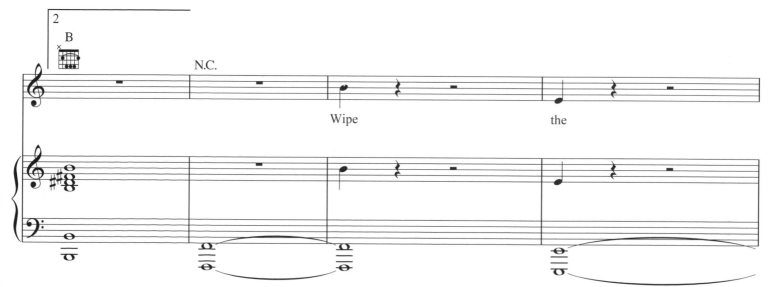

Wipe the

lust from your eyes. I see

that you're not mine. I can see the lust in your eyes. You can't

Fmaj7   Em7

hide ___ it. ___ You can't be the one I re - ly, we're di -

Fmaj7   Em7

N.C.   D.S. al Coda

CODA   B

vid - ed. ___

TRUE COLORS

Words and Music by ABEL TESFAYE, MAGNUS AUGUST HOIBERG,
BENJAMIN LEVIN, BRITTANY HAZZARD, JACOB DUTTON,
WILLIAM THOMAS WALSH and SAMUEL WISHKOSKI

Recorded a half step higher.

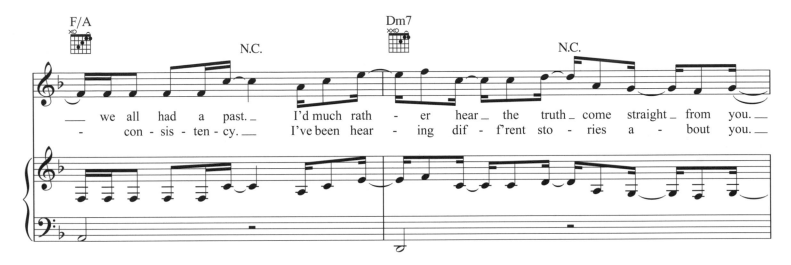

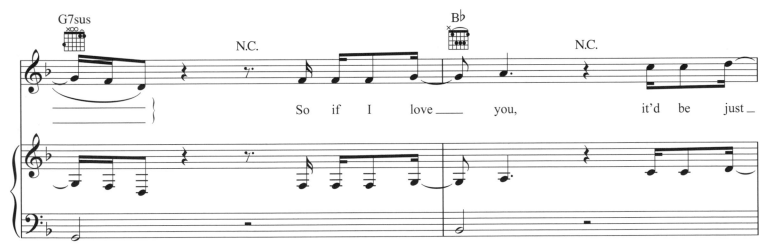

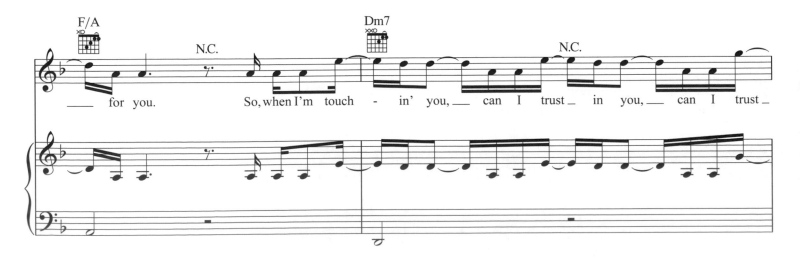

in you, oh, ___ ba - by? Girl, come show me your true col - ors.

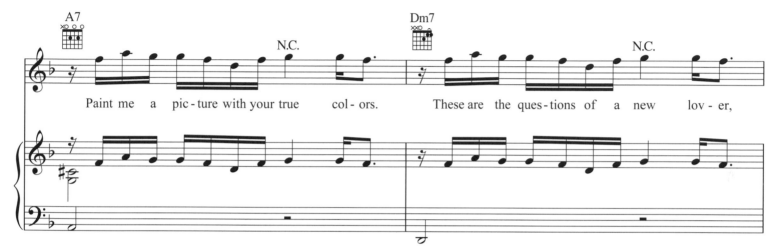

Paint me a pic - ture with your true col - ors. These are the ques - tions of a new lov - er,

truc col - ors, true ___ col - ors. Girl, come show me your true col - ors.

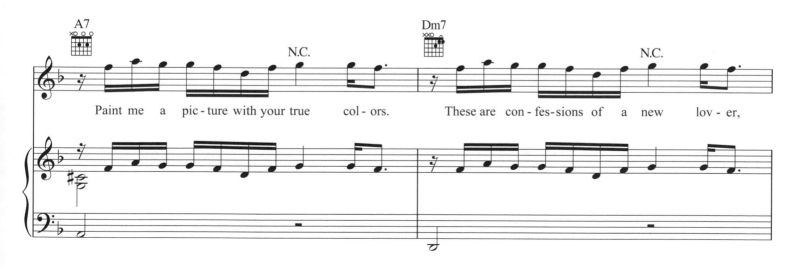

Paint me a pic - ture with your true col - ors. These are con - fes - sions of a new lov - er,

true col - ors, true _____ col - ors. true col - ors. Ba - by, show me you're a

keep - er. _____ It's been hard for me to keep up. _____ You've been try'n' to keep me

in the dark, _____ but, ba - by girl, I see you. _____ Ba - by, show me you're a

see you. _____

see you. _____ Girl, come show me your true col - ors.

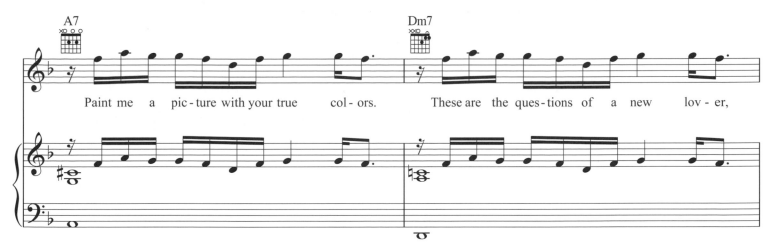

Paint me a pic-ture with your true col-ors. These are the ques-tions of a new lov-er,

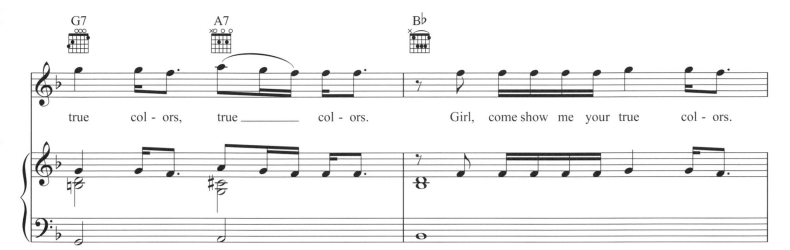

true col-ors, true col - ors. Girl, come show me your true col - ors.

Paint me a pic-ture with your true col-ors. These are con-fes-sions of a new lov-er,

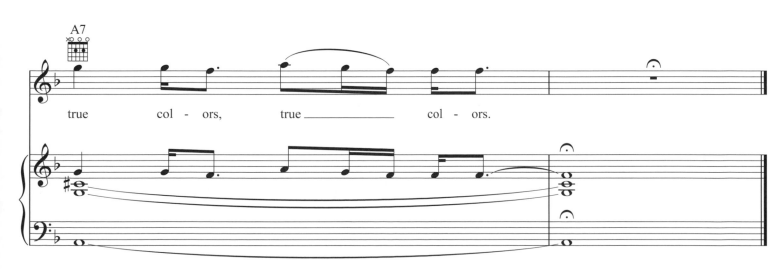

true col - ors, true col - ors.

STARGIRL INTERLUDE

Words and Music by ABEL TESFAYE,
MARTIN McKINNEY, ELIZABETH GRANT
and TIMOTHY McKENZIE

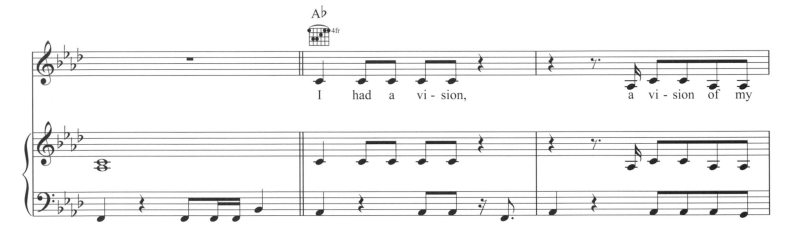

I had a vi-sion, a vi-sion of my

nails in the kitch-en, scratch-ing coun-ter tops, I was scream-ing,

my back arched like a cat, my po-si-tion could-n't stop you were hit-tin'. And

I should-n't cry, but I love it, Star - boy. ___

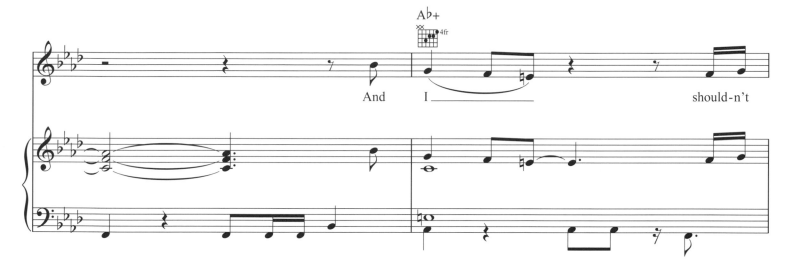

And I ___ should-n't

cry, but I love it, I love it, Star - boy. ___

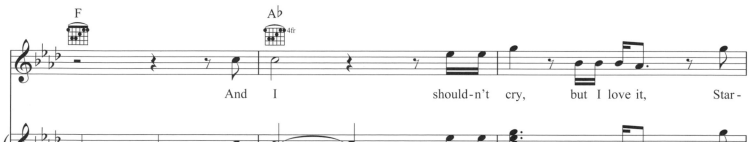

And I should-n't cry, but I love it, Star-

boy. ____ And I _____ should-n't
cry, but I love it, Star - boy. ____

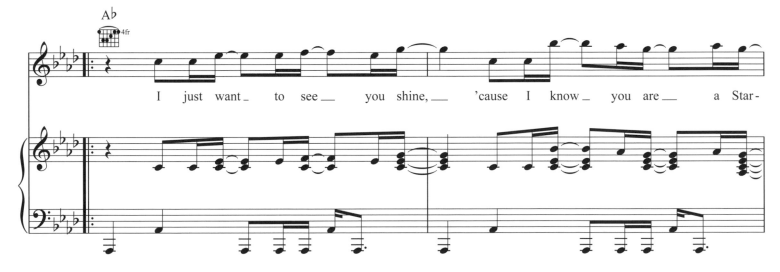

I just want _ to see __ you shine, __ 'cause I know _ you are __ a Star-

Repeat and Fade

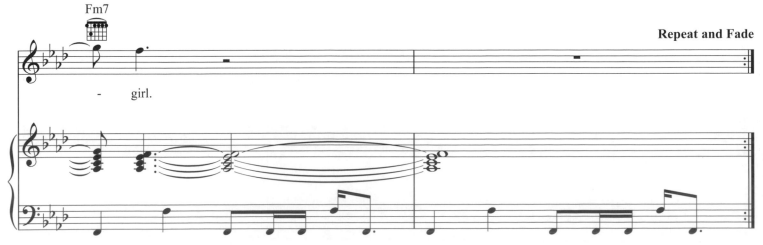

\- girl.

SIX FEET UNDER

Words and Music by ABEL TESFAYE, HENRY WALTER,
MARTIN McKINNEY, NAYVADIUS WILBURN, LELAND WAYNE,
JASON QUENNEVILLE, AHMAD BALSHE and BENJAMIN DIEHL

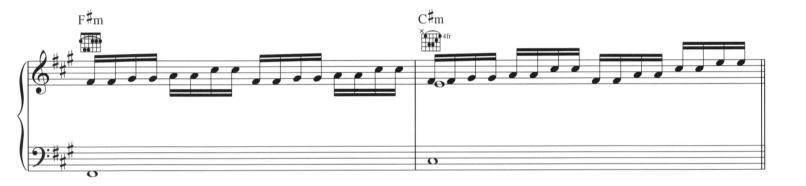

Ask a-round a-bout her. She don't get e-mo-tion-al.

Kill off all her feel - ings, _____ that's why she ain't ap - proach - a - ble. _____

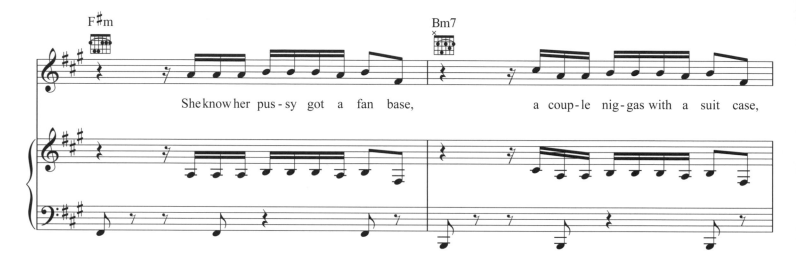

She know her pus - sy got a fan base, a coup - le nig - gas with a suit case,

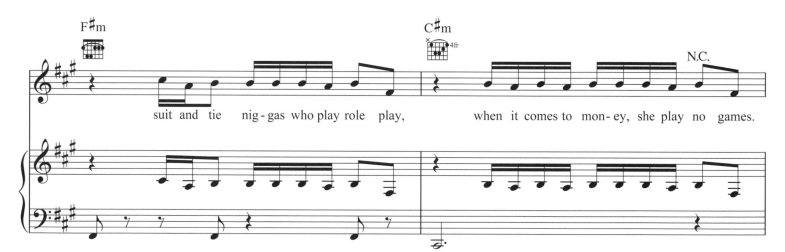

suit and tie nig - gas who play role play, when it comes to mon - ey, she play no games.

She lick it up just like a can - dy, _____ she wan - na make them leave their fam - 'ly. __

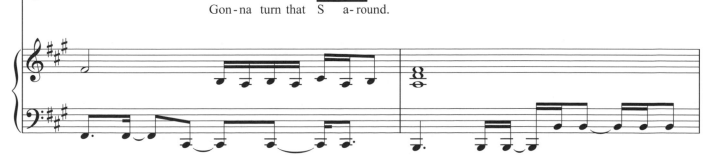

F#m
C#m

mind.   She ain't gon - na lose her   mind _____   till she

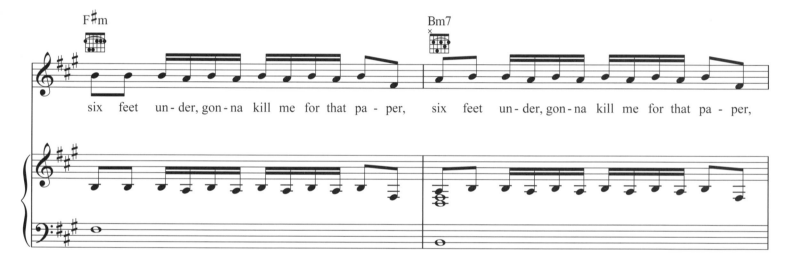

F#m
Bm7

six   feet un - der, gon - na kill me for that pa - per,   six   feet un - der, gon - na kill me for that pa - per,

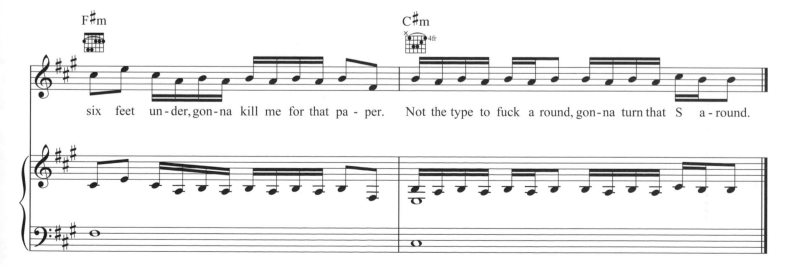

F#m
C#m

six   feet un - der, gon - na kill me for that pa - per.   Not the type to fuck a round, gon - na turn that S a - round.

SIDEWALKS

Words and Music by ABEL TESFAYE, MARTIN McKINNEY,
DANIEL WILSON, ROBERT JOHN RICHARDSON,
KENDRICK LAMAR and ALI SHAHEED JONES-MUHAMMAD

Moderately slow

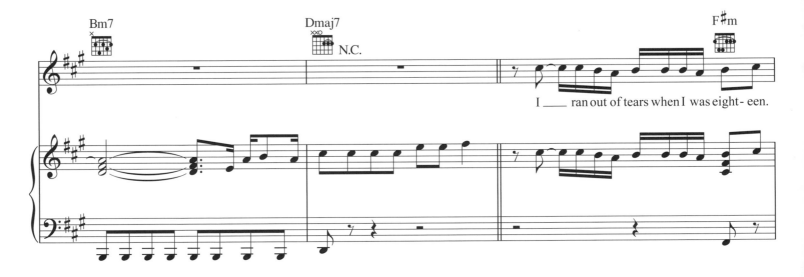

I ___ ran out of tears when I was eight- een.

So, ___ no-bod- y made me but the main streets. 'Cause ___ too man- y peo- ple think they made me,

But they lead ___ me on. _____

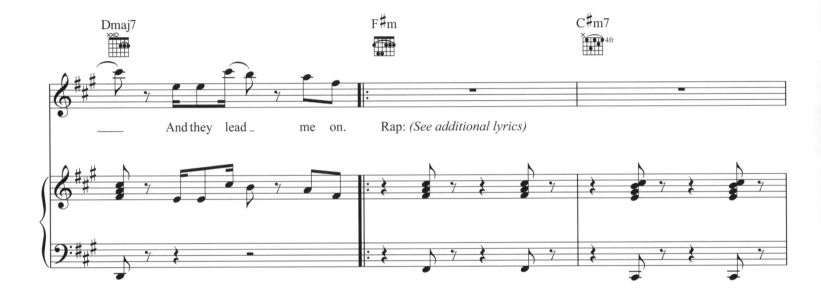

___ And they lead ___ me on.   Rap: *(See additional lyrics)*

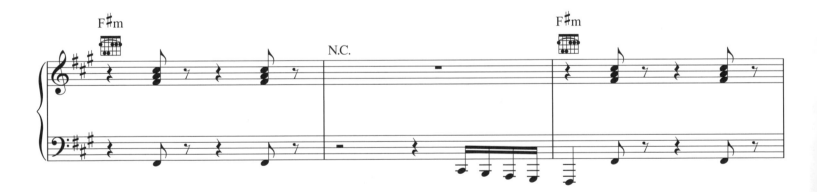

and they lead me on.

Additional Lyrics

Rap: Say, say, say
I come from murder one, brung late night melee
Say, say, say
We hung all summer, sprung mattress with bae bae
Say, say, say
Trippin' off Dyke, and my name strike with pay day
Say, say, say
Flippin' blue lightning, tightening, strapped with AK
Say, say, say
OG one, told me one, show me one, eight ways
How to segue
Pussy, power, profit in headache
I reminisce my life innocence
Or life innocent
Or life intimate, with fame
Light limo tint
With light women, dark women in it
Awe Kenny, good game
She wanna hang with a Starboy
The sun and the moon and star, boy
Astronomer, anonymous
I line 'em up, grind 'em up, there's nine of us
And five of us are probably fucked
She mollied up, I tallied up all the parts, boy
Twenty legs, arms, head (head)
Head, head, more head (head)
Oh God, bless the dead (yah)
I'm livin' life, high off life
I wear my chokes off to bed
I'm the greatest nigga, why you scared to say it?
I wanna rock, I wanna rock, I wanna cop more land
I never stop
I wanna quick advance on a bill if it ain't one
Break everything, I'm a hustler, came from

LOVE TO LAY

Words and Music by ABEL TESFAYE,
ANDERS SVENSSON, MAX MARTIN,
SAVAN KOTECHA, AHMAD BALSHE
and ALI PAYAMI

Moderately fast

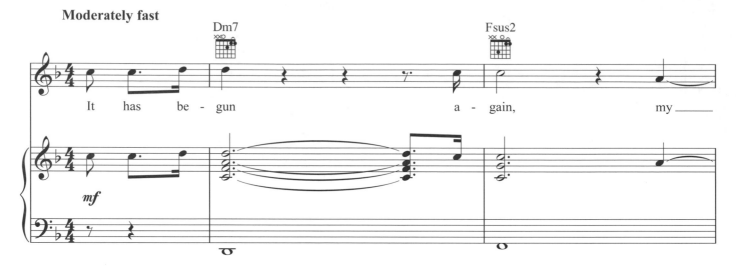

It has be-gun a-gain, my ____

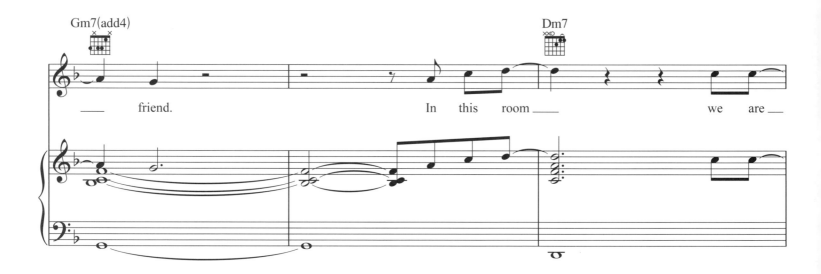

____ friend. In this room ____ we are ____

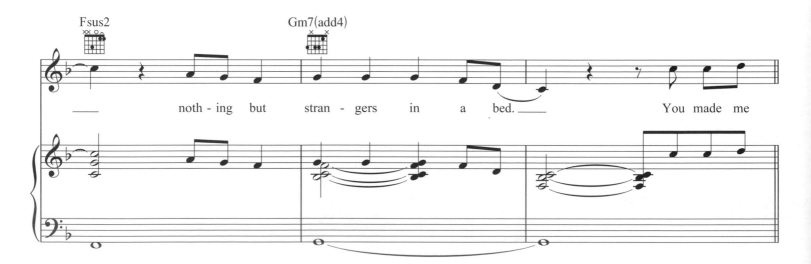

____ noth-ing but stran-gers in a bed. ____ You made me

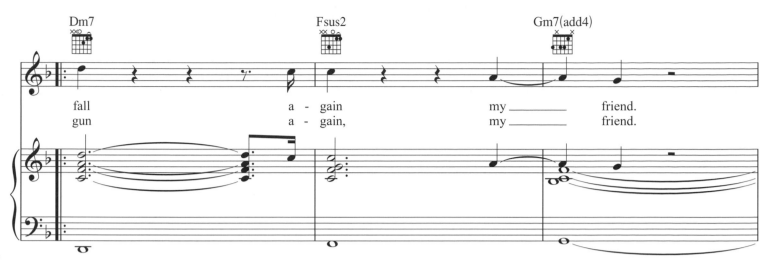

fall a - gain my _____ friend.
gun a - gain, my _____ friend.

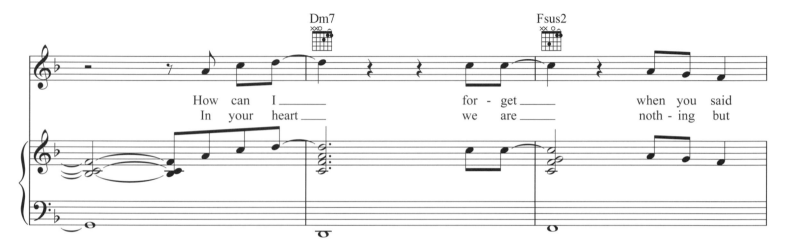

How can I _____ for - get _____ when you said
In your heart _____ we are _____ noth - ing but

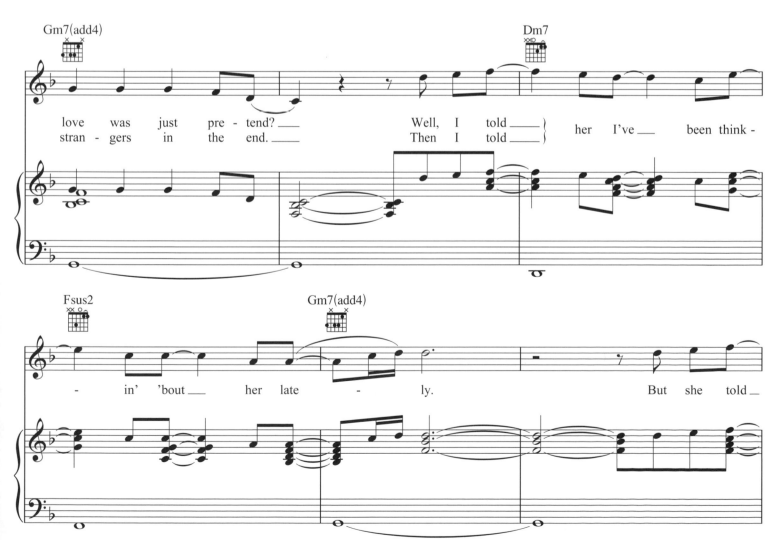

love was just pre - tend? _____ Well, I told _____ her I've _____ been think -
stran - gers in the end. _____ Then I told _____

- in' 'bout _____ her late - ly. But she told _____

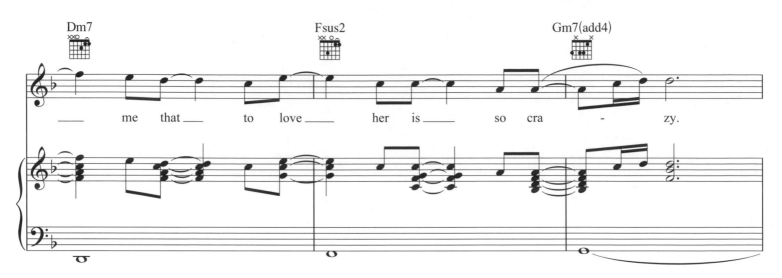

_____ me that _____ to love _____ her is _____ so cra - zy.

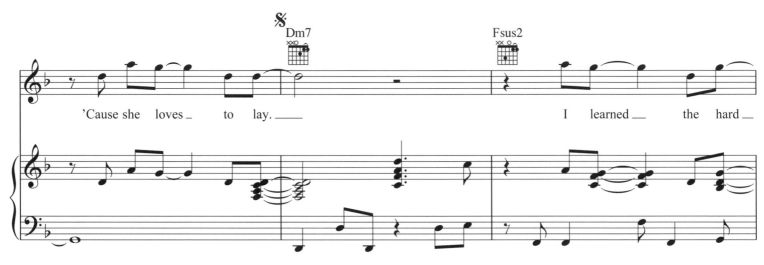

'Cause she loves _ to lay. _____ I learned _____ the hard _____

_____ way. _____ She loves _ to lay. _____ I'm all _____ to blame.

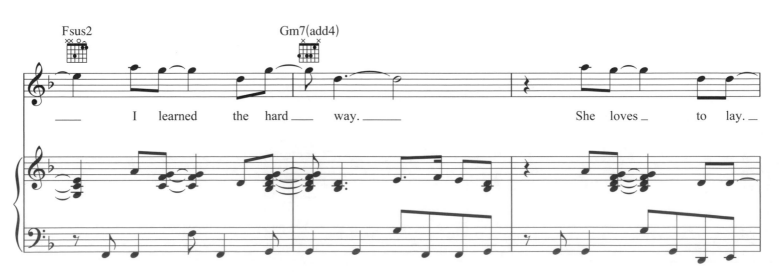

_____ I learned the hard _____ way. _____ She loves _ to lay. _

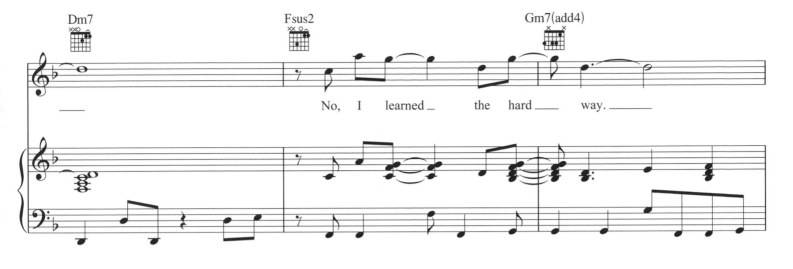

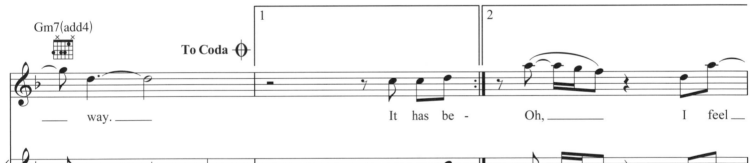

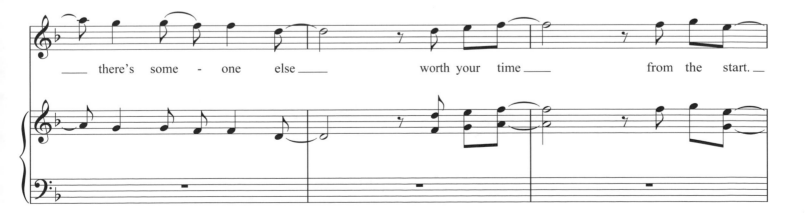

He's just ____ one call ____ a - way ____ from your mind ____
and your heart. ____ It has be -

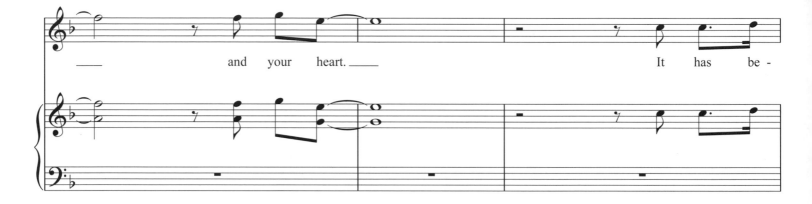

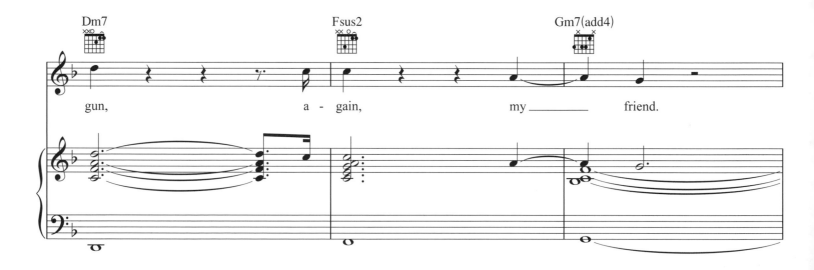

Dm7   Fsus2   Gm7(add4)

gun, a - gain, my _____ friend.

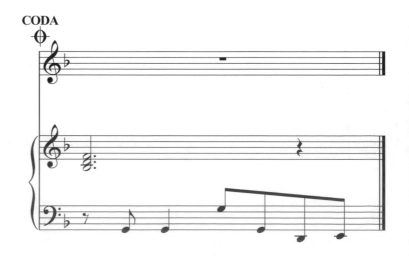

D.S. al Coda   **CODA**

She loves ____ to lay. ____

A LONELY NIGHT

Words and Music by ABEL TESFAYE,
ANDERS SVENSSON, MAX MARTIN,
SAVAN KOTECHA, AHMAD BALSHE,
ALI PAYAMI and JASON QUENNEVILLE

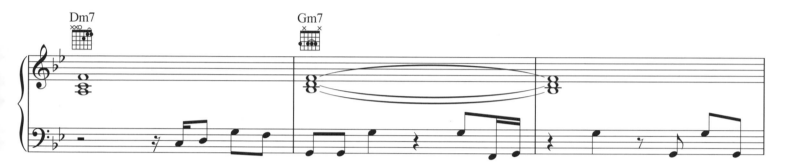

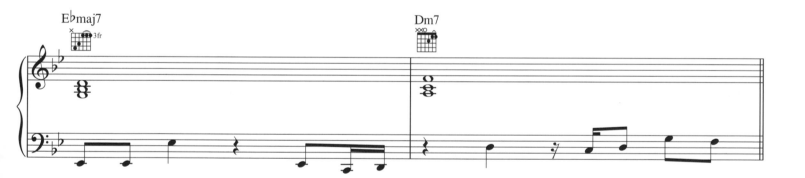

Why would you wan-na bring some-thin' be-tween us? There's noth-in' be-tween___

How can I make you re-think your de-ci-sion, un-rul-y de-ci-

E♭maj7   **Dm7**

___ us,   oh.
- sion?   Oh.

Gm7

Why would you wan - na use a life to keep us, to keep us to - geth -
What's gon - na make you re - think your po - si - tion? I know your in - ten -

E♭maj7   **Dm7**

- er?   Oh,   oh.
- tions,   oh,   oh.

Gm7

Bet - ter when we're both a - part,   bet - ter when we're both a - part. We're no

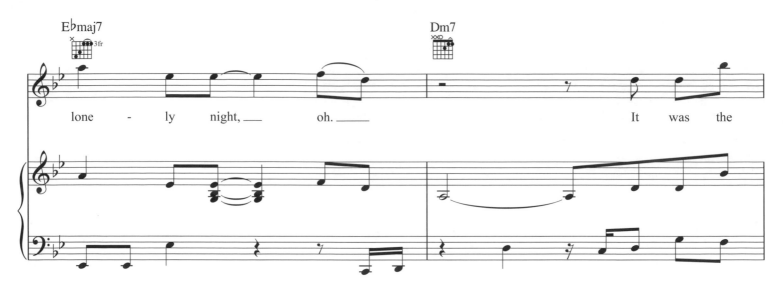

lone - ly night, __ oh. __ It was the

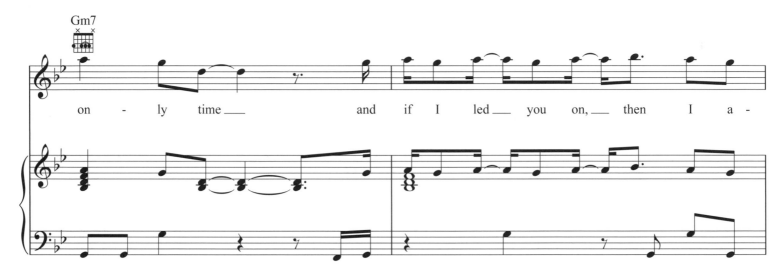

on - ly time __ and if I led __ you on, __ then I a -

pol - o - gize, __ oh. __

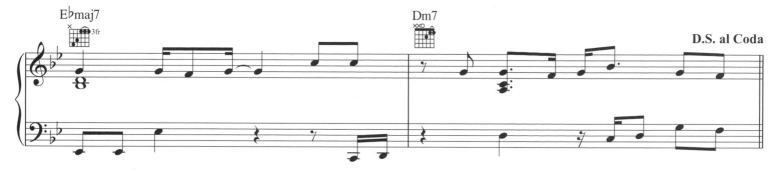

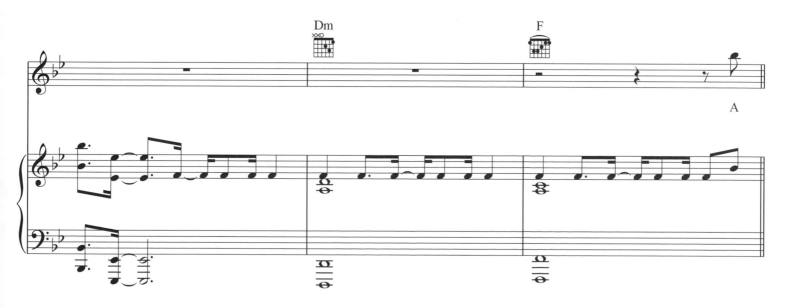

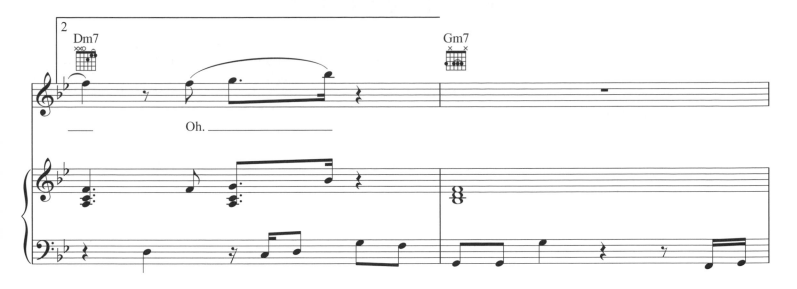

Oh. _____

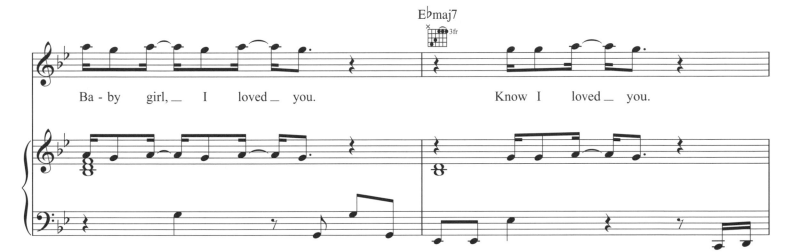

Ba - by girl, __ I loved __ you.   Know I   loved __ you.

Know I   loved __ you. _____

Repeat and Fade

ATTENTION

Words and Music by ABEL TESFAYE,
MAGNUS AUGUST HOIBERG, BENJAMIN LEVIN,
ADAM KING FEENEY, WILLIAM THOMAS WALSH
and MUSTAFA AHMED

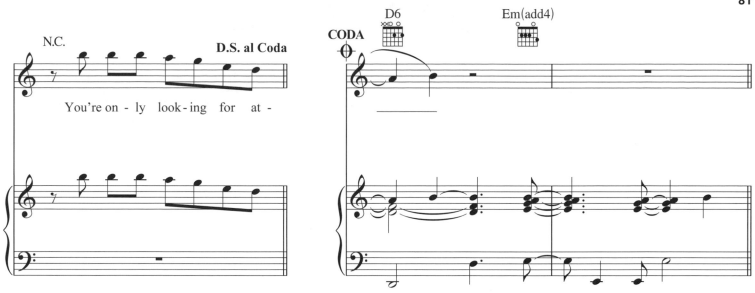

You're on - ly look-ing for at -

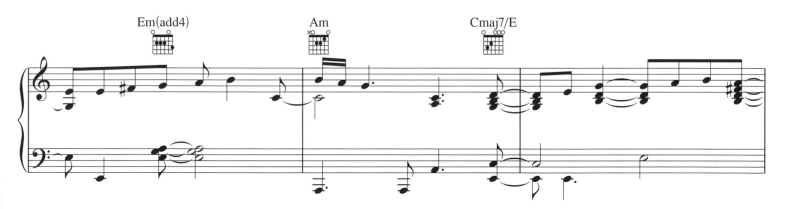

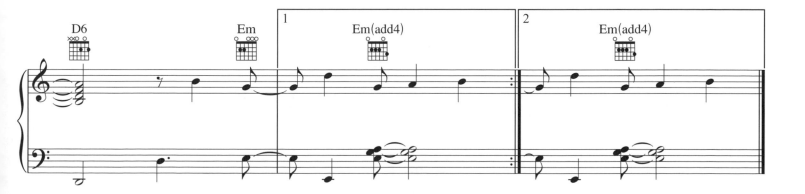

ORDINARY LIFE

Words and Music by ABEL TESFAYE, HENRY WALTER,
MARTIN McKINNEY, ANDERS SVENSSON,
MAX MARTIN, SAVAN KOTECHA,
AHMAD BALSHE and ALI PAYAMI

Moderately slow

Whoa, _ whoa, whoa, _ whoa, ___ whoa, _

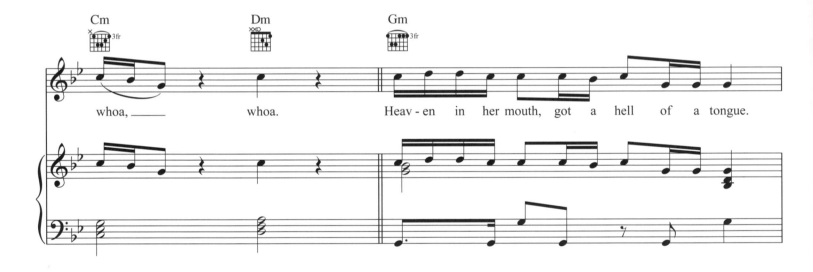

whoa, ___ whoa. Heav- en in her mouth, got a hell of a tongue.

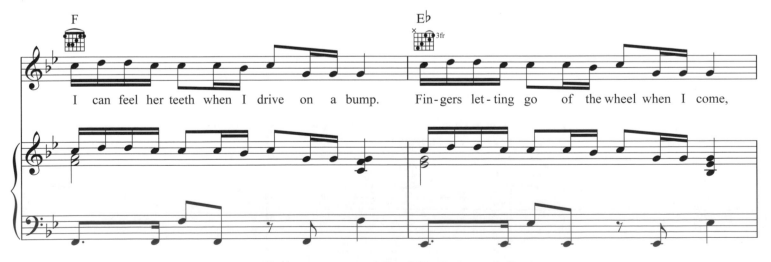

I can feel her teeth when I drive on a bump. Fin- gers let-ting go of the wheel when I come,

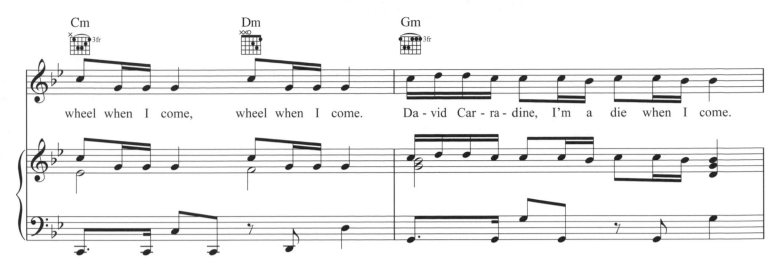

wheel when I come, wheel when I come. Da - vid Car - ra - dine, I'm a die when I come.

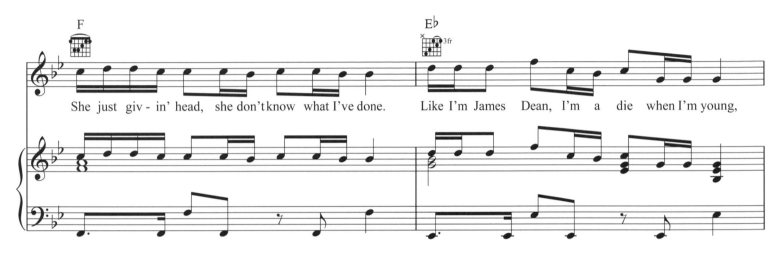

She just giv - in' head, she don't know what I've done. Like I'm James Dean, I'm a die when I'm young,

die when I'm young, die when I'm young. ___ Heav - en knows that I've been told ___

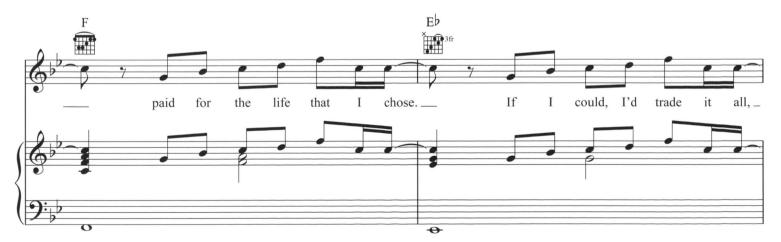

___ paid for the life that I chose. ___ If I could, I'd trade it all, ___

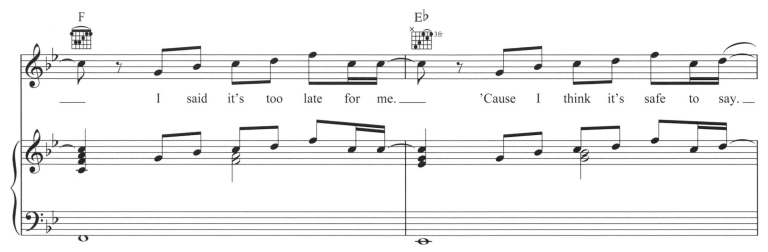

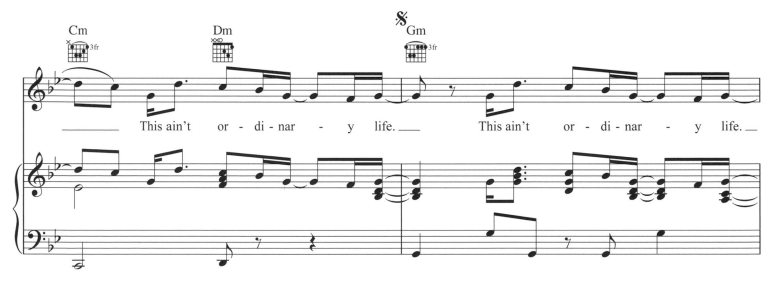

no or - di - nar - y life.___ This ain't or - di - nar - y life.___

___ This ain't or - di - nar - y life.___ This ain't or - di - nar - y life.___

To Coda ⊕

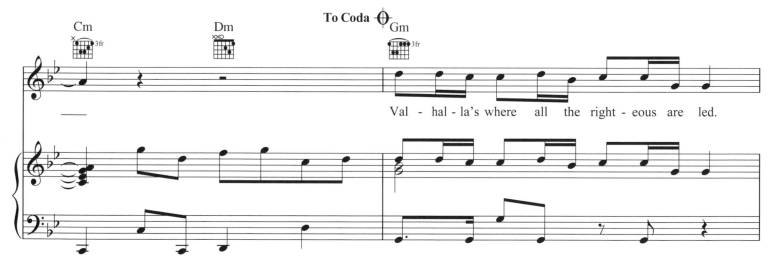

___ Val - hal - la's where all the right - eous are led.

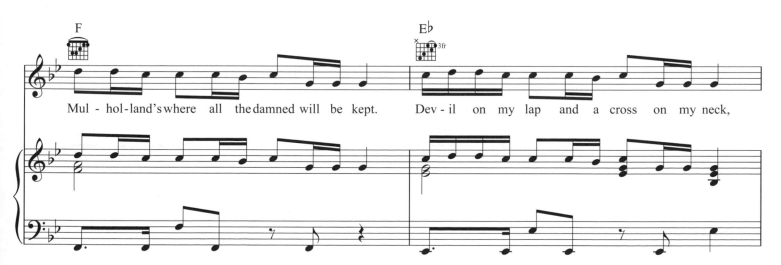

Mul - hol - land's where all the damned will be kept. Dev - il on my lap and a cross on my neck,

cross on my neck, cross on my neck. O- ver for - ty - five, I'm a drift on a bend,

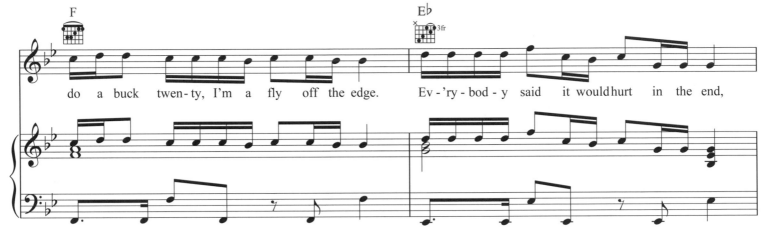

do a buck twen- ty, I'm a fly off the edge. Ev -'ry - bod - y said it would hurt in the end,

hurt in the end, but I feel __ noth - in'. She said that she'll pray for me. __

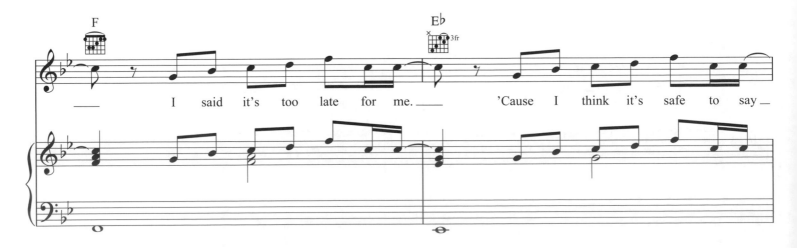

__ I said it's too late for me. __ 'Cause I think it's safe to say __

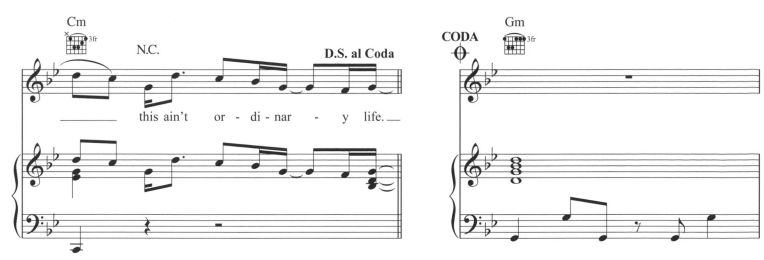

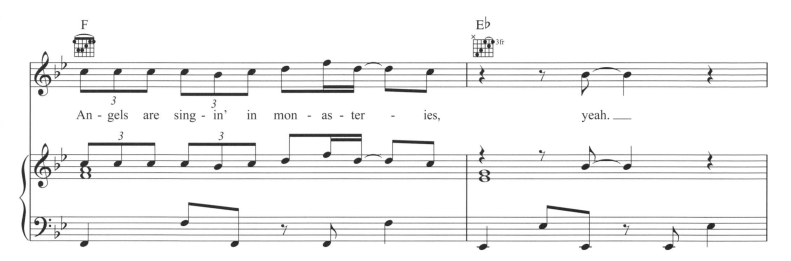

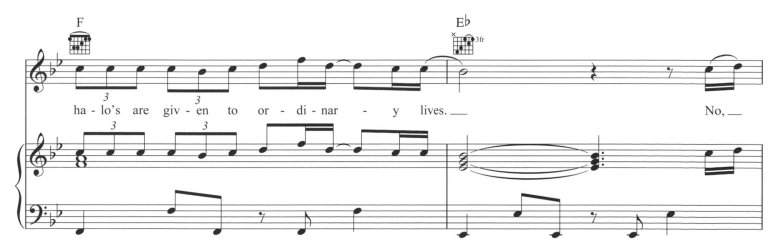

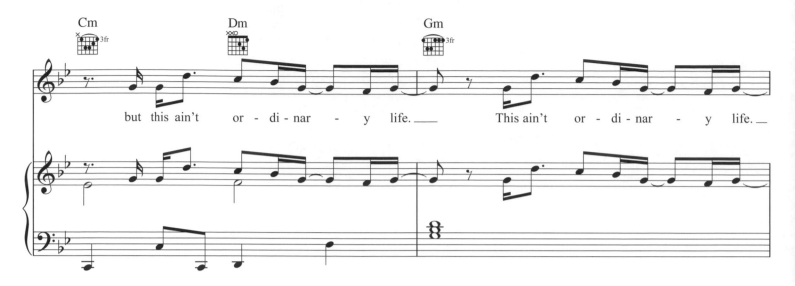

but this ain't or - di - nar - y life. ___ This ain't or - di - nar - y life. ___

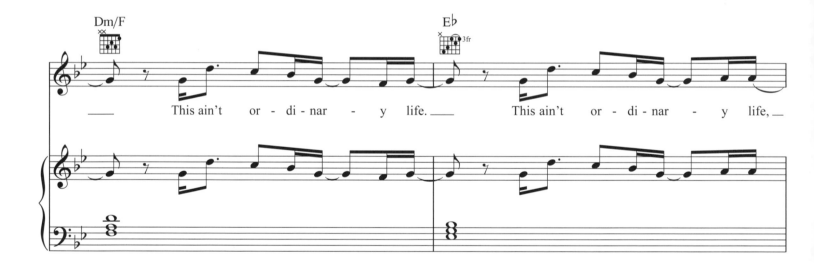

___ This ain't or - di - nar - y life. ___ This ain't or - di - nar - y life, ___

___ no or - di - nar - y life. ___ This ain't or - di - nar - y life.

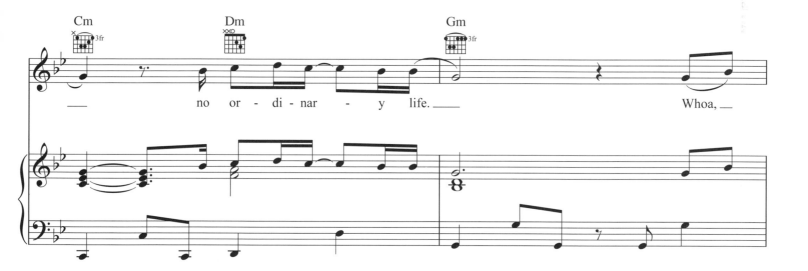

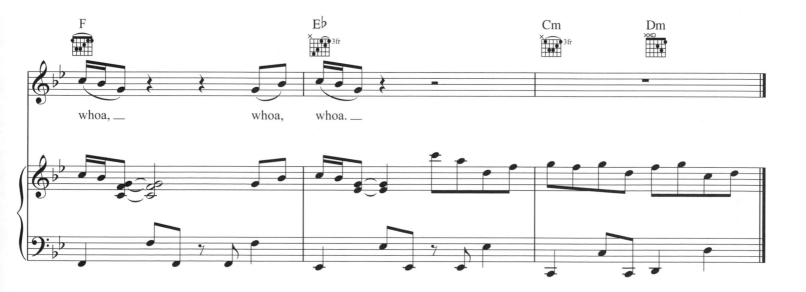

NOTHING WITHOUT YOU

Words and Music by ABEL TESFAYE,
THOMAS PENTZ, HENRY WALTER,
JASON QUENNEVILLE, AHMAD BALSHE
and BENJAMIN DIEHL

*Recorded a half step higher.

out you, __ with-out you. __ Noth - ing, __ noth - ing, __

noth - ing, __ noth - ing __ with - out __ you.)

ALL I KNOW

Words and Music by ABEL TESFAYE,
MAGNUS AUGUST HOIBERG, NAYVADIUS WILBURN,
AHMAD BALSHE and BENJAMIN DIEHL

Moderately

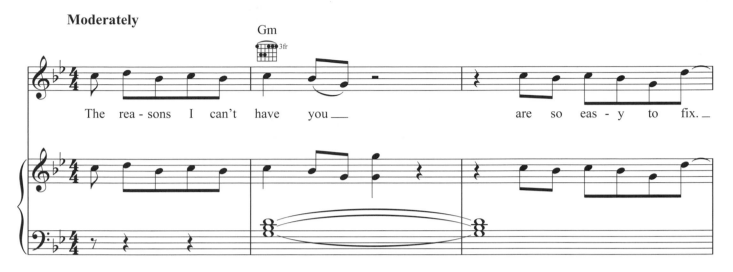

The rea-sons I can't have you ___ are so eas-y to fix. ___

___ I did-n't real-ly plan to, ___

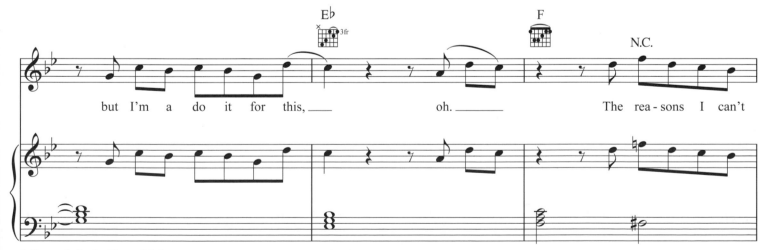

but I'm a do it for this, ___ oh. ___ The rea-sons I can't

* Recorded a half step higher.

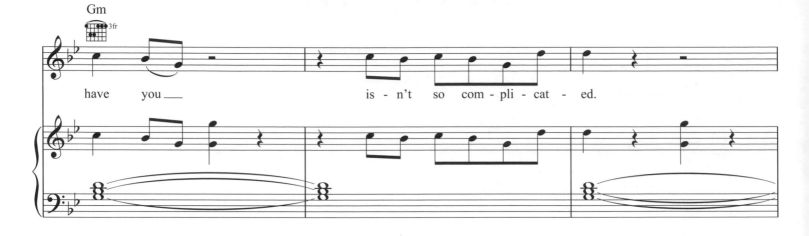

have you _____ is - n't so com - pli - cat - ed.

N.C.   Gm

Ba - by, if you _____ let me, _____ I _____ won't _ hes - i - tate, _____

Eb   F   N.C.   Gm

_____ tate. _____ All I know, _

all I know is this,   all I

know, ____ all I know is this. _____

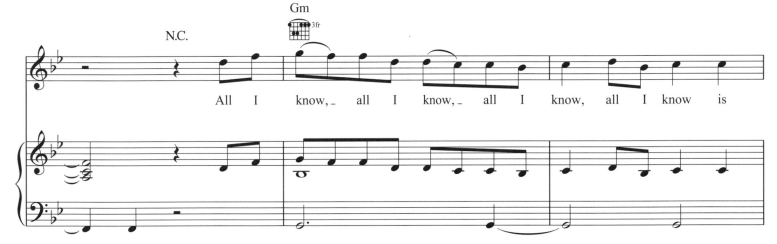

All I know, ___ all I know, ___ all I know, all I know is

this. ___ All I know, ___ all I know, ___ all I

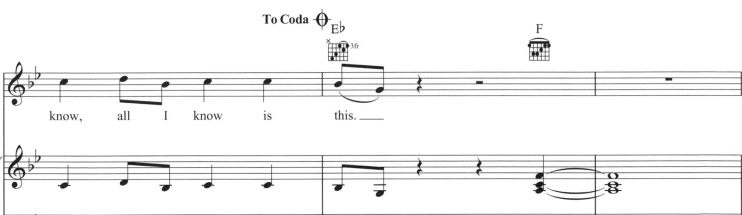

know, all I know is this. _____

I know there's been stig-ma 'round me._____ I know you heard

things a-bout me._____ You sleep one eye closed.

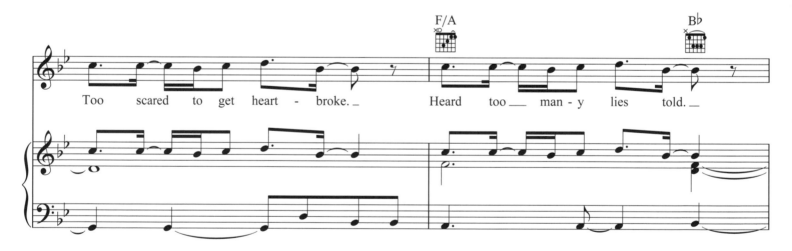

Too scared to get heart-broke.__ Heard too__ man-y lies told.__

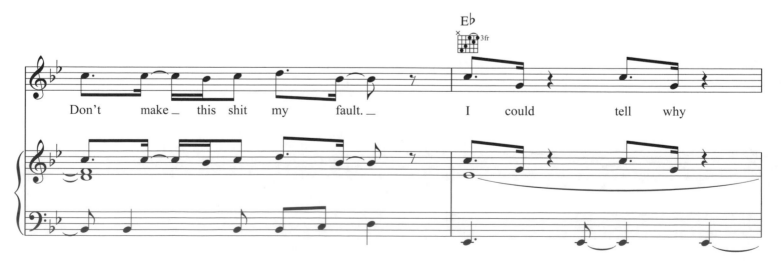

Don't make__ this shit my fault.__ I could tell why

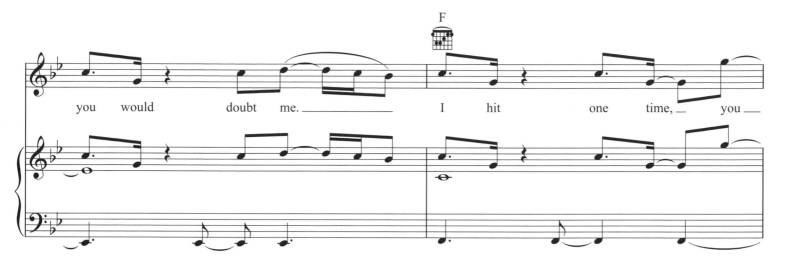

you would doubt me. _____ I hit one time, __ you __

__ can't live with-out me. ___ Girl, I'm just peak-in', I'm __

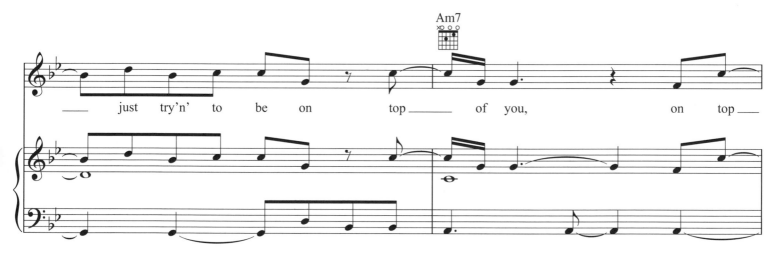

__ just try'n' to be on top ___ of you, on top __

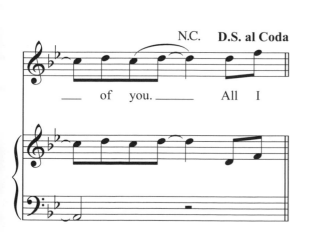

__ of you. ___ All I

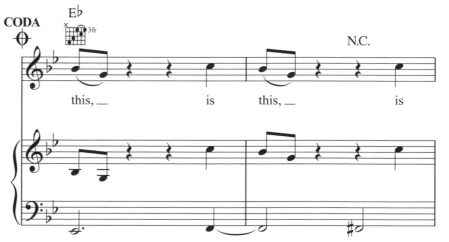

this, __ is this, __ is

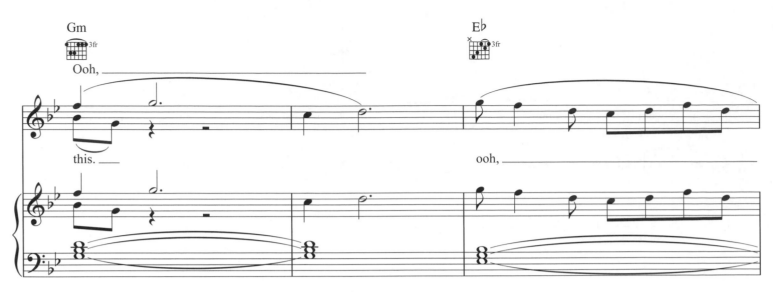

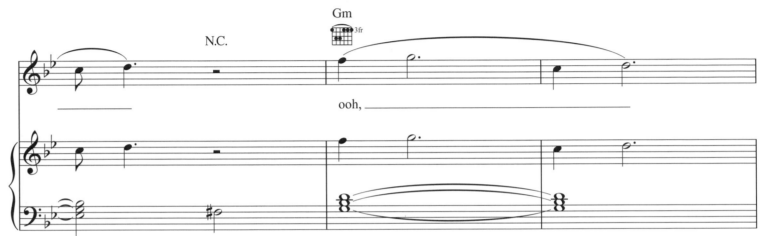

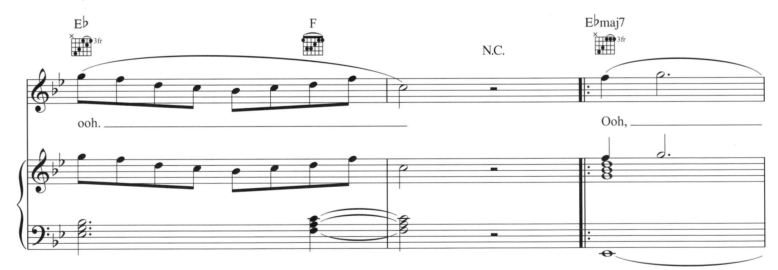

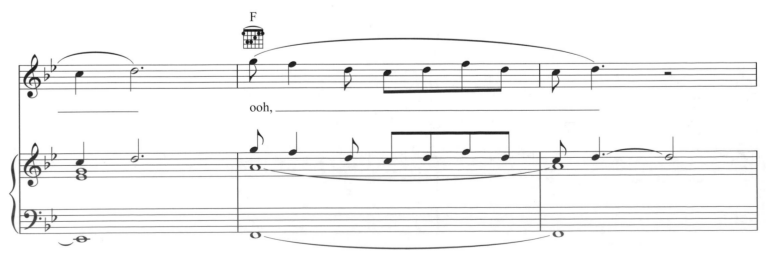

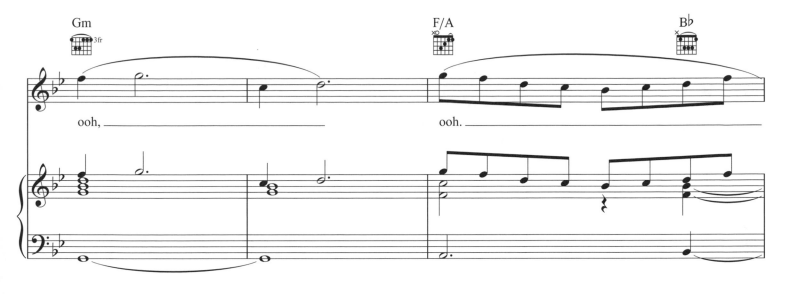

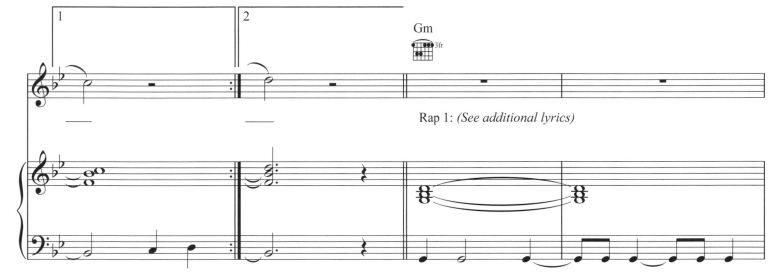

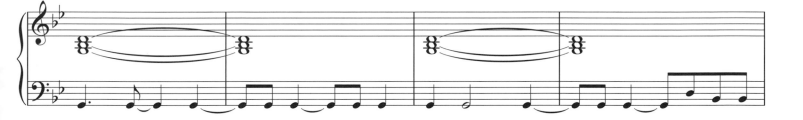

Rap 1: *(See additional lyrics)*

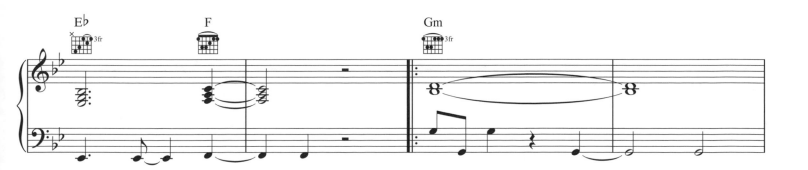

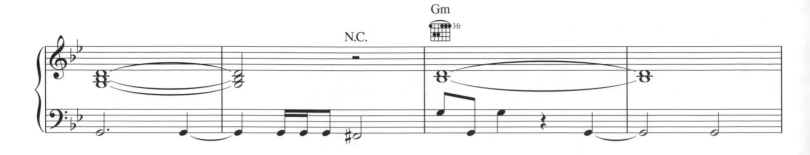

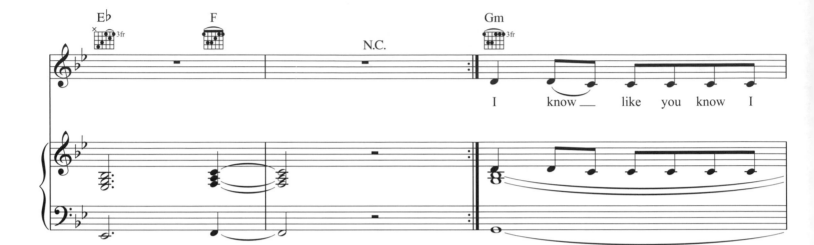

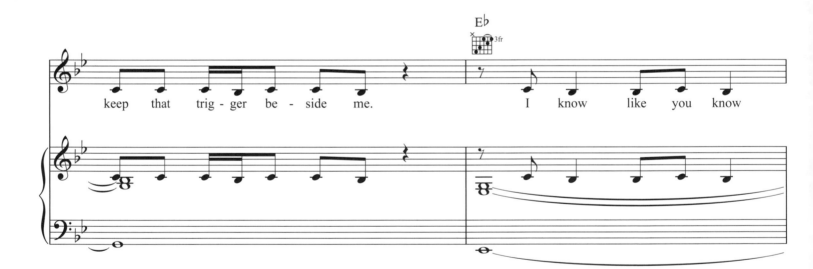

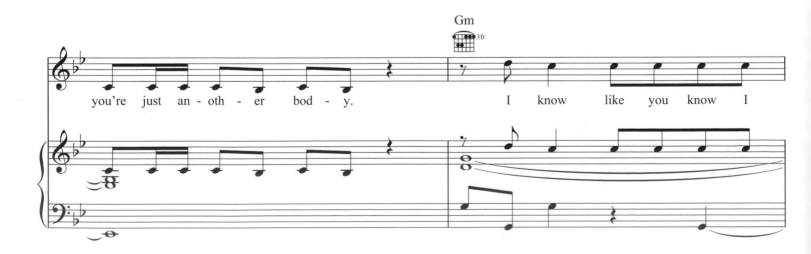

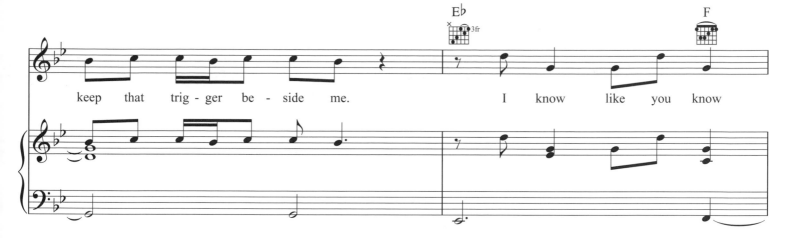

keep that trig - ger be - side me. I know like you know

you're just an - oth - er bod - y. Ooh, _____

Rap 2: (*See additional lyrics*)

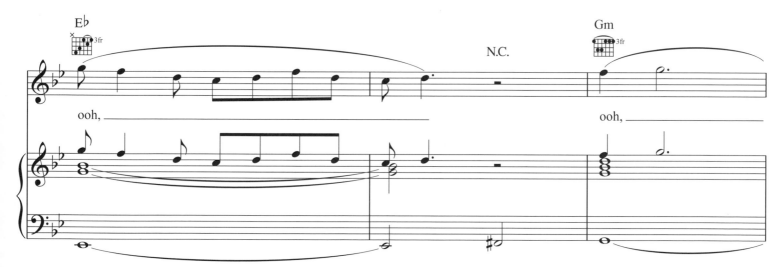

ooh, _____ ooh, _____

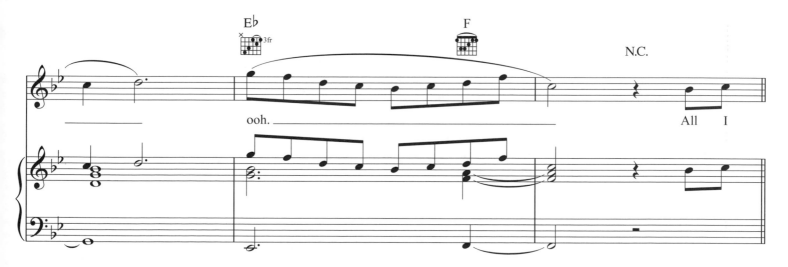

_____ ooh. _____ All I

Additional Lyrics

Rap 1: She, she, sleep with one eye open (yeah)
I'm terrified to get my heart broke (wha up)
Blood talkin' like a Piru (ay)
Fuck with me, nigga, gon' die slow (gang)
Lamborghini make you Crip walk (skrt)
I'm splashin' off with my side hoe (ay)
Full of these medicals, bitches, got several (yeah)
She eat the dick up like it's an edible
Then I get back to my capital (pour)
I got the Glock on the passenger (pour up)
I got these tropical fantasies (woo)
They gon' remember my legacy (pour up)
Hang out the roof of the Ghost (yeah)
The cash in my pocket spill right on the floor (yeah-yeah)
The cash in my pocket spill out in the floor (hold up)
When the cash overflow, let the cash overflow
I done fucked a bitch that boogie (yeah)
Have you ever, ever fucked a bitch that boogie? Woah-oh (yeah yeah)
I done fucked a bitch that boogie
I done, I done , I done fucked a bitch that boogie, woah oh
I done fucked a bitch conceited
I done fucked a few, few bitches conceited
We just wanna say we did it
We just wanna say we did it (XO)

Rap 2: Have you fucked a bitch this pretty? (yeah)
Hit her on the first night and went and bought titties (yeah, yeah)
Have you fucked a bitch this pretty? (yeah)
Hit her on the first night and went and bought titties
Niggas always sneak dissin' (yeah)
We gon' continue fuckin' they bitches (oh yeah)
I ain't just fucking that bitch
I been all the way up, makin' love to that bitch

I FEEL IT COMING

Words and Music by ABEL TESFAYE,
ERIC CHEDEVILLE, GUY-MANUEL DE HOMEM-CHRISTO,
THOMAS BANGALTER, HENRY WALTER
and MARTIN McKINNEY

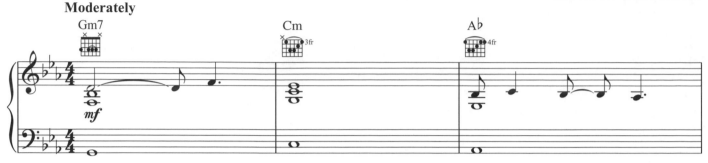

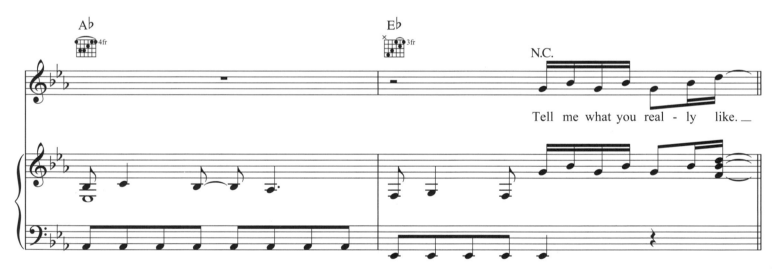

Tell me what you real - ly like.

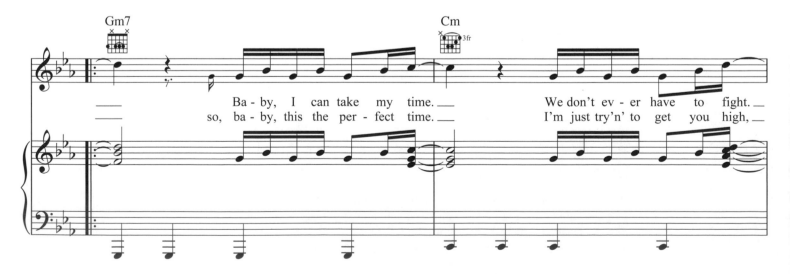

Ba - by, I can take my time. ___ We don't ev - er have to fight. ___
so, ba - by, this the per - fect time. ___ I'm just try'n' to get you high, ___

Just take __ it step __ by step. I can see it in your eyes, __
ba - by, off __ this touch. __ You don't need a lone - ly night. __

'cause they nev - er tell me lies. __ I can feel that bod - y shake __
Ba - by, I can make it right. __ You just got - ta let me try __

and the heat __ be - tween __ your legs. __ You've been scared of
to give __ you what __ you want. __

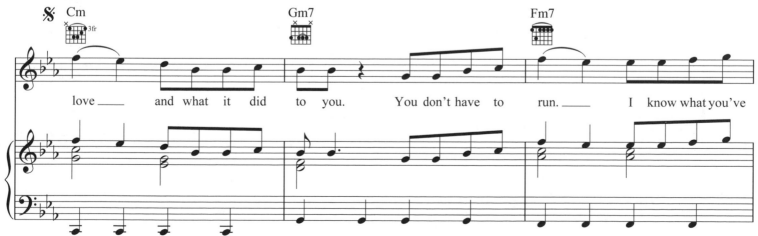

love __ and what it did to you. You don't have to run. __ I know what you've

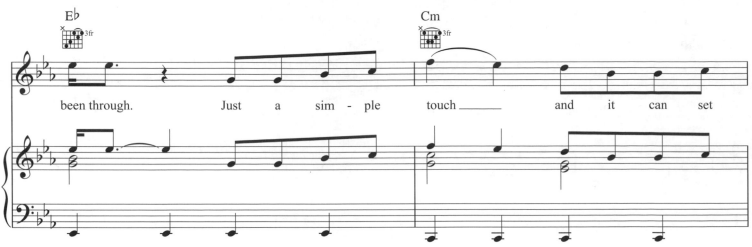

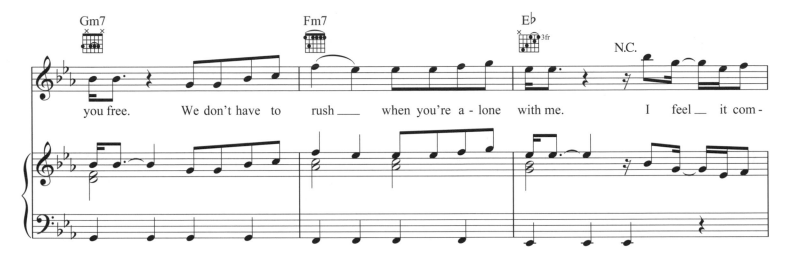

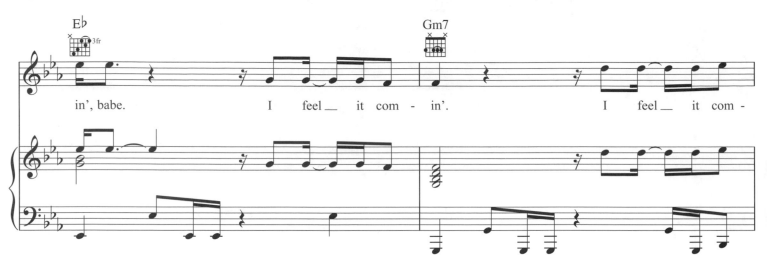

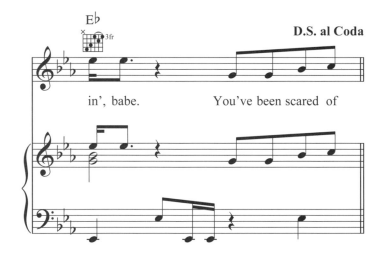

in', I feel __ it com - in', babe. I feel __ it com-

in', I feel __ it com - in', babe. I feel __ it com-

in', I feel __ it com - in', babe.

Repeat and Fade

I feel __ it com - in', babe.

DIE FOR YOU

Words and Music by ABEL TESFAYE,
MAGNUS AUGUST HOIBERG, MARTIN McKINNEY,
DYLAN WIGGINS, WILLIAM THOMAS WALSH
and PRINCE 85

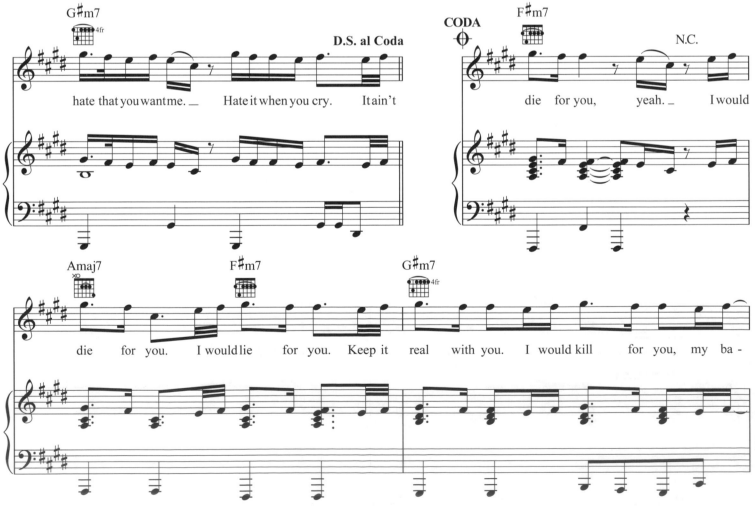